Contents

Introduction   7

1. A Nation of Wine Drinkers   9
2. Winemaking with Grape Concentrates   15
3. Minimum Equipment   25
4. Beginners' Bloomers   37
5. How to Make and Blend your Daily Wine   43
6. How to make Burgundy, Beaujolais, Chianti, Hock, Moselle, Champagne and other Regional Wines   55
7. How to Fool the Wine Snobs   85
8. The Legal Position   91
9. Sherry, Port, Vermouth, Madeira and Other Stronger Wines   95
10. Poor Man's Whisky, Gin, Brandy and Liqueurs   111
11. Advanced Winemaking   123
12. Home Brewing   139
13. Cooking with Wine   151
14. Let's End with a Party   171

Epilogue   183

Metric Conversion Tables   184

Glossary   185

Index   189

For Ted

Wine Man's Bluff

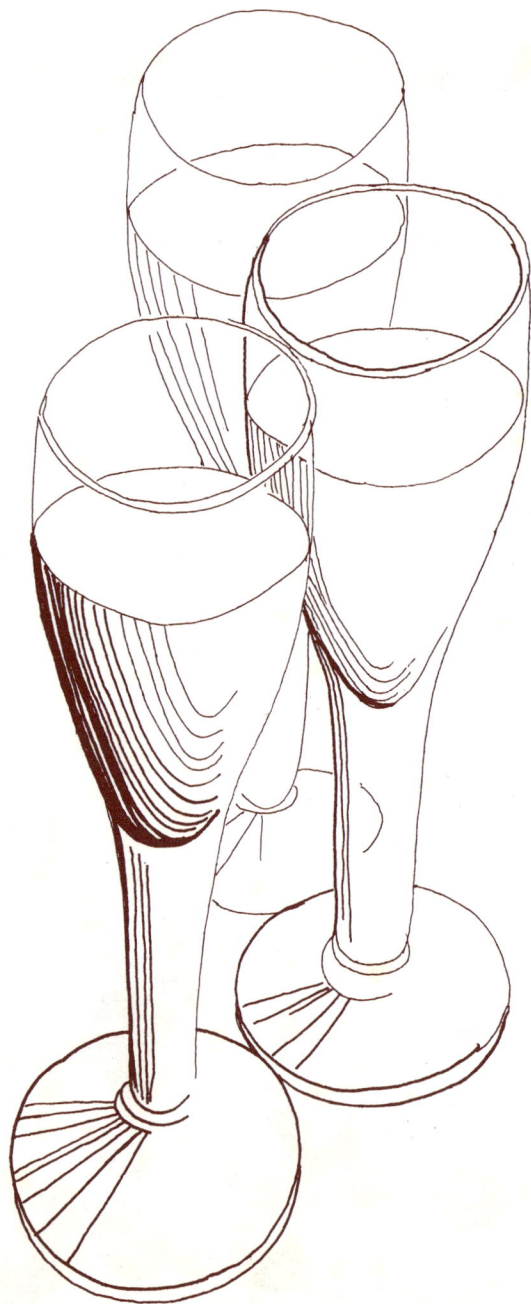

Wine Man's Bluff

Phoebe Hichens

with illustrations by Sally Clare

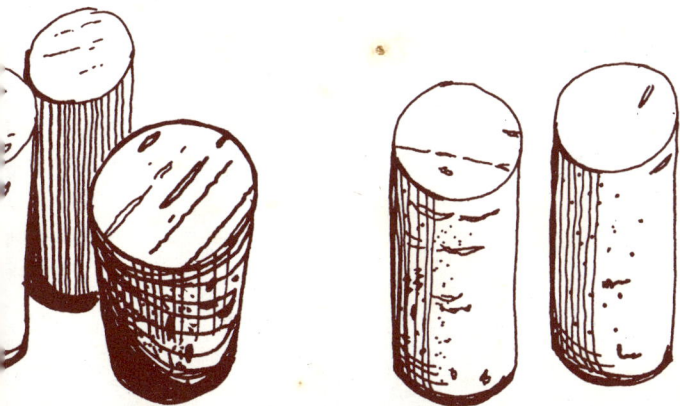

Macmillan

SBN 333 14981 5

First published 1973 by
MACMILLAN LONDON LIMITED
London and Basingstoke
Associated companies in New York
Dublin Melbourne Johannesburg and Madras

Printed in Great Britain by
JOLLY AND BARBER LIMITED
Rugby

Graphic design by John Richards
Illustrations by Sally Clare except as indicated below.

The author and publishers are grateful for permission to reproduce
the H. M. Bateman drawings on pages 86, 88 and 90, to the artist's
daughters, Mrs Ernest Willis and Mrs Michael Pine, and to
George Harding for the diagrams on pages 32 and 98.

Introduction

This book is for people who love the true grape wines, from countries like France, Germany, Italy and Spain.

If you are interested in the old country recipes, based on local dandelions and elderberries and beetroot and so forth, read no further. There are many excellent tomes on the subject, but nothing to help you here. If, however, you are interested in making true grape wines for a few pence a bottle: if you want to make them fast – ready for drinking in four to six weeks: and if you would like the process to be so mess-free and fuss-free, that it can be done as easily in a small city flat as in an ample country house – then this book is very much for you.

There is no need to feel that the wines you know and love can only be produced in other countries. A month from now, you could be drinking a Vin Ordinaire so like the wines you drink abroad, that no one will dream it's homemade.

Drink no longer water,
but use a little wine
for thy stomach's sake
and thine often infirmities

I *Timothy,* v 23

1. A Nation of Wine Drinkers

A Nation of Wine Drinkers

We might as well face the fact that we are turning into a nation, and perhaps even a world of wine drinkers.

For many people it has all happened quite recently; and, like as not, started with those first adult holidays in France or Italy or Spain. The sunshine was seductive, and so was the fact that any restaurant, however small and unpretentious, assumed that you would be drinking wine with your meal. Indeed jugs of the local vintage would often appear on the table before they had even been ordered. So how could you avoid discovering that the two things, food and wine, belong together in a delightful, almost an inevitable way? From then on, your eating and drinking life could never be the same, not even when the sun vanished and the rain rained and the holiday felt a thousand years ago. You couldn't un-learn the conviction that wine is a natural and necessary accompaniment to every meal, including Monday lunches. (Perhaps particularly Monday lunches.)

The next discovery follows almost automatically, and it is that wine belongs in the cooking just as naturally as it belongs with the meal. And it belongs, not only in exotic dishes, but in run-of-the-mill casseroles, jellies, fruit salads, haddock pies and other daily dishes. A wine bottle by the stove becomes as basic as a wine bottle on the table.

We shouldn't feel sinful about this, for daily wine – in moderation of course – is recommended by health experts. It usually contains some iron, and by dilating the blood vessels, it improves circulation and brings blood to aid the digestive processes in the stomach. Appetites are sharpened, tense muscles are relaxed and – because the digestion is working better – the physical enjoyment of food is heightened. Even St Paul, who is not noted for debauchery, could urge Timothy to take a little wine for the sake of his stomach.

It's reasonable, therefore, to feel that a regular glass with meals is doing oneself a favour; but what it is doing to one's budget is quite another matter. Even if you comb every available cellar for bargains, even if you buy the plonkiest plonk, the cost of daily wine turns out to be appalling; and, according to the wine merchants, this is likely to get worse rather than better.

For many years now siren voices have been murmuring – 'how would you like a fine full-bodied wine at a fraction of the usual price?' But tempted as you may have been to become a winemaker in your own kitchen, there were probably a lot of prejudices for you to overcome. Homemade cakes and jam are fine, but homemade *wine* arouses instant suspicion among the more sophisticated drinkers. Isn't it bound to be sweet and sticky and tasting of something quite inappropriate like parsley? All right for Women's Institutes and antique villagers, but not the thing for people who like real wine, wine that tastes like wine? There are, of course, some good reasons for this prejudice. The traditional English wine recipes tend to come out extremely sweet: partly because our forebears thought in terms of dessert rather than of table wines: partly because they knew sugar acted as a preservative and this was important in their less hygienic days: and perhaps they had a

sweeter tooth than us anyway. It is also true to say that the old recipes do not produce anything like the wines we sipped on the banks of the Rhine or the streets of Montmartre. How can they? The basic ingredients are English fruits, flowers and vegetables, with flavours nothing like the hot sun grape. You can't blame a wine for tasting of parsley if it's made of parsley.

Nevertheless, critics of homemade wine are missing the point – which is that *we* don't have to follow in the grandmotherly footsteps. The present range of grape concentrates (which will be discussed fully in the next chapter) has opened up new possibilities for the amateur winemaker: principally the possibility of producing wines reminiscent of France and Germany and Italy and other countries associated in most peoples minds with the grape.

'But it's all so difficult and messy and time-consuming.' This is another common reaction, and some of the more conventional books on winemaking have done plenty to encourage it. They don't make anything sound easy, still less quick; and when they start in on the scientific background, it can be really alarming. Some people may take it in their stride when they read that concurrent and consecutive oxidation, reduction and esterification reactions are part of the maturing processes in a wine. They may even know what is meant by a 1×5 cc bulb type class B pipette for testing the acidity of a must. But one can't help feeling that the average beginner would prefer to hear how winemaking can be made simple, if not foolproof.

This book will try to answer questions which seem relevant to our present day tastes and living conditions and time schedules. Questions like:

Can you make wine in a London flat? or a Liverpool bedsitter?

Would you be mad to offer it to your grander friends?

Can it be made drinkable in weeks rather than months and years?

Must it be kept at exactly the right temperature – and what happens if you don't have an airing cupboard?

The problems of time and space are indeed crucial. We are drinking wine faster than ever before, but we probably don't have room in our homes for endless casks and jars and bottles. Some home vintners may still be willing to follow recipes involving forty pounds of fresh fruit and eight years maturing in wood; but many others will feel that if the winemaking is to make sense, the process must be simple and the turnover brisk.

This can be done. A few gallons of wine can be started in less time than it takes to cook the dinner, and they can be finished and ready for drinking four to six weeks from the day they began. No – I'm not pretending that this is the ideal way to produce wine, and I haven't forgotten that young wines will usually taste thin and raw and acid. But things can be done which overcome the problems. You can add more instant taste and smoothness by adding extra grape sugar. And you can blend with older wines, fruitier wines, stronger wines. Such wines may well have to be bought so this will add to the cost; but if you blend in the right way, the quantities of bought wine will be kept to a minimum and the price of your own vintage will still be astonishingly economical.

Exact instructions will be given in a later chapter on the extra grape sugar and the blending with commercial wines, so all that need be emphasised here are the two basic points:

1) You can produce in four to six weeks a most drinkable Vin Ordinaire: one that costs between 15p and 20p a bottle and compares very well with commercial brands priced around 75p.

2) There are better ways to make better wines, of course, and these will also be discussed.

It must also be said that this book is confining itself, unashamedly, to the grape wines; and although recipes will include other ingredients, they will all be chosen with the object of aiding and abetting the main grape flavour. This is not because the old country wines, made from dandelions and nettles and beetroot and so on, are bad – on the contrary, they can be extremely good, and anyone who is interested in them will find there are many excellent books on the subject. But it is a fact that *people like the tastes they are used to.* (If you don't believe this, ask any food manufacturer or any distiller or any cigarette firm.) They like new washing powders and gadgets and cars and cosmetics, but not new flavours. And it is also a fact that we are becoming more and more devoted to grape wines if only because these are the ones we've been brought up on, these are the ones we are used to.

Perhaps the most important point about this book is that it has not been dominated by the taste and experience of one winemaker. The first step was to find out what wine drinkers really want – 'I like what I know, but I'd like it to cost a quarter as much' – was in most cases the comment which summed it all up.

And the second step was, not just to experiment on my own, but to see what a real cross-section of winemakers had to contribute. Obviously I talked to the experts who take the classes, who sell the equipment, who write the books, who win the competitions. But also it seemed necessary to talk to the nice fallible people who understood – totally – the troubles of the amateur because they'd fallen into all the usual traps themselves: stuck fermentations, odd flavours, overflowing air-locks, cloudy colours and the like. Maybe they didn't even understand the workings of a hydrometer, let alone a 1×5 cc bulb class B pipette. The result of these investigations should make sense to all beginners, and also to the many many winemakers who have tried and given up in disgust. Modern cookery books have shown how good meals can be adapted to our lives, homes, tastes, budgets; and the first thing to grasp is that winemaking can be exactly the same.

Going Metric

The British can be a stubborn people, and it is generally agreed that they are not going to abandon their old system of weights and measures overnight. Apart from anything else, it would involve throwing out a lot of our existing kitchen – and perhaps winemaking – equipment; and life is expensive enough without that.

With decimalisation of the currency we had no choice; but no one can force us to start measuring in kilogrammes rather than pounds, or in litres rather than pints. Sooner or later it will happen, but the process is likely to be gradual, even slow, and we have decided not to force the pace in this book. All recipes use the old system.

However, it is not realistic to ignore the future, and basic conversion tables appear on page 184.

2. Winemaking with Grape Concentrates

Winemaking with Grape Concentrates

The basic process of making wine is the same, whatever ingredients you use; and reduced to the essentials, it is a very simple process indeed. The three vital elements are:

Sugar
Water
Yeast

and once these are put together, the process called fermentation begins.

Fermentation means that sugar and yeast react with each other, and the sugar is converted into alcohol. Sweetness is lost as the alcoholic strength rises, so that a straight sweet liquid can become a dry alcoholic liquid – i.e. wine.
Wine made with plain sugar will not, of course, have much flavour; and winemakers have always preferred to use ingredients like fruit or flowers or vegetables which contain a) natural flavour and b) natural sugar. Granulated sugar or honey can be added to supplement the 'natural' sugar and the amount of this will depend on the strength and sweetness desired in the final wine. For example: a dry table wine with an alcoholic content of around 10% will require a total of about 2 lb of sugar (natural and added) for every gallon of liquid.

The right level of sugar is one of the basic essentials in winemaking. Too much will give the yeast indigestion and stop it functioning at all: too little will mean that there is not the wherewithal to create sufficient alcohol: and finally, yeast cannot survive after a certain level of alcoholic strength has been reached, and any sugar that remains in the liquid after this point will remain as residual sweetness. This may not matter if you want a sweet wine; but it is obviously undesirable if you are aiming for dryness.

These facts may sound a bit formidable, but there is really nothing to worry about. It's dead easy to calculate the right amounts of sugar when wines are based on grape concentrates (see page 33) and even if you do get it a little wrong, the chapter on blending will show you how to put it right.

Another fact, basic to winemaking, concerns temperature. Yeast works slowly when the temperature falls below sixty-five degrees Fahrenheit, and will probably become inactive at fifty degrees or under. It works more briskly when the temperature rises into the upper sixties, and is probably at its most vigorous between seventy and eighty degrees. Anything higher, however, may kill it outright. This means that fermenting wine has to be kept in a consistently warm place, as near to seventy degrees as you can make it. Not every home can provide the ideal solution but again, don't worry: there's always a way round, as the chapter on Minimum Equipment will show.

The last 'basic' is the container for fermenting wine. Oak casks are the best; but as these are expensive to buy and laboursome to clean, they can't be recommended for beginners. Glass jars are perfectly satisfactory, and so – with one reservation – are plastic buckets and bins. A recent report has shown that coloured plastics contain toxic chemicals which may be absorbed by the fermenting wine or beer. (Yellow plastic is particularly suspect.) So, to be on the safe side, always buy white plastic or line your container with a transparent or white polythene bag. Never use any kind of metal.

So now let's suppose you are about to make your first gallon of wine, using a can of grape concentrate. You know the principles: the actual procedure could hardly be more straightforward.

The Basic Winemaking Method

First Step

Take a small screw-top bottle – a Schweppes 8 oz non-returnable tonic water bottle is ideal – and fill half-full of blood-heat water. Add two rounded teaspoonfuls of wine yeast and shake well. Put the bottle in a warm place for six hours.

This is called 'activating' the yeast and means that it will go to work much more quickly and efficiently when you add it to the grape juice.

Second Step

Empty the contents of the grape concentrate can into a white plastic bucket or one with a white or transparent polythene liner, and make up to a gallon of liquid with blood-heat water.

Third Step

Stir in the yeast mixture from the screw-top bottle, cover the bucket with a lid, polythene or an ordinary cloth. Put in a warm place (for instance in an airing cupboard) or anywhere close to 70°F and leave for three days.

Fourth Step

Add supplementary sugar. (The amount, as I said earlier, will depend on the type of wine required.) This sugar should first be dissolved in a little warm water and then added to the bucket. Leave for a week.

Fifth Step

Pour the wine from the bucket into a glass gallon jar, using a large kitchen funnel. Discard sludge and cloudy liquid at the bottom of bucket. Top up the jar with cold water, plug the neck with cotton wool and move to a cooler place (at room temperature). Leave for three weeks, after which the wine will be ready for bottling.

Remember, this is only the basic procedure, using only the basic ingredients and equipment. As you will probably have guessed, many refinements and variations are possible – as, for example, 'siphoning' the wine into the jar instead of pouring it, boosting fermentation with yeast nutrient, adding sugar little and often instead of all at once. These will all be discussed in due course; but for the moment, we are dealing with the bare essentials of winemaking and grape concentrates.

Why should one use grape concentrates? Wine can, in fact, be flavoured with almost anything. We are told that our ancestors used to throw dead rats and mice into the fermenting liquid on the grounds that it gave the wine body; and there were others who found that an agreeable pungency came with the addition of old socks. Taste is an interesting thing. In general, though, there has always been a prejudice in favour of grapes; and the reasons for this are convincing.

Grapes are one of the best balanced fruits in existence. They contain all the things conducive to a good wine flavour, and, what's more, contain them in ideal proportions; so they start off with a big taste advantage over other ingredients. Many sugars are capable of fermenting, but some ferment better than others – and grape sugar best of all. You are likely to get a much better reaction from the yeast when the wine is based on grapes. Lastly, grape wines are much more efficient at clearing themselves than wines made with other ingredients. The latter will often need help from chemicals like pectozyme, or wine finings; but the grape variety end up a clear brilliant colour without any such aid.

Grapes are ideal – but for the amateur winemaker they present difficultties. Not every country can grow their own; or if they do, the sun may not be hot enough to produce the right level of grape sugar. (This is true of the English sun.) Imported grapes are expensive, and it's hard to know if they are the right type for a burgundy, or the right type for a hock, or whatever it is you want to make. As a final disincentive, the business of extracting juice from any quantity of grapes is excessively messy.

Concentrates are a compromise, and they do have certain drawbacks. Nevertheless, they come as an enormous blessing to the winemaker who is also a grape addict because, for the first time, they make it possible for us to produce the type of wines we know and like. And, as I've already made clear, that is what this book is all about.

The words 'grape concentrate' describe pretty well what the product is – namely, a quantity of grapes which have been processed to reduce the water content. This is done by a form of heat treatment which extracts liquid, condenses bulk, but retains all the sugar and other essential properties of the fruit. Grapes are processed in the country where they are grown, and the strained concentrate is imported into England.

A very wide range of concentrates is now being offered. There are the straight red and white concentrates which are the cheapest, and which don't claim to make any specific type of wine. And then there are concentrates to make all the familiar names: burgundy, beaujolais, chianti, hock, chablis, moselle, sauternes, graves, sherry, port, vermouth and so on. This is not to say that the grapes necessarily come from the area where, traditionally, a certain wine is made. Sometimes they do – the Chianti concentrate brought out by Continental Wine Experts uses grapes from Tuscany – but as a general rule, they don't. When you buy a can, say, of Red Bordeaux Type concentrate, the grapes are far more likely to have come from Spain or Cyprus than Bordeaux: they may even have come from somewhere as unexpected as China.

The concentrate has, however, been carefully balanced and certain elements, like tannin or citric acid, added so that it comes as near as possible to the traditional grape. Some firms, like CWE and Unican, add these extras in synthetic form with laboratories and scientists dedicated to getting the balance exactly right. Unican, for instance, employ a micro-biologist and a team of six technicians to work on these aspects. Southern Vinyards achieve the desired balance by blending different juices: Mr Instone, their managing director, tells me that they import juices from no less than sixteen countries and that he relies on taste rather than laboratory tests – ultimately his own taste. One still wonders, of course, why it has to be done in this way and why the firms can't simply import the right grapes from the right place; but there seem to be some very good price reasons for this which will be discussed in a minute.

First of all, though, let's take a look at the various brands of grape concentrate. These are becoming more numerous every day and the budding winemaker may be puzzled which to choose: you may know that you want to make a beaujolais-type wine, but you will soon discover that there are several beaujolais-type brands available, and the price differences between them can be substantial. I have done some research to try and make an assessment of the different brands, particularly in relation to their prices; but it must be emphasised that the results are neither complete nor final. Prices fluctuate, new brands keep appearing, and the whole sales area keeps expanding so fast that any judgement can quickly be outdated.

The following are the brands generally available:

CWE (Continental Wine Experts)
Unican
Boots
Southern Vinyards
Garrigos
Sparklets
Vinopak
Solvino
Hidalgo
Fermenta

In a few years this list may have doubled or trebled; but nevertheless, I have been able to draw some general conclusions which may be of help to the beginner.

More expensive concentrates
It doesn't follow that the grape concentrate is better just because it costs more. The price difference can arise from the fact that the grapes come from an expensive country, like France, rather than an inexpensive one, like Rumania.
The idea of French grapes is, of course, very attractive and it would be easy to believe that the quality would justify a higher price; but this is not necessarily the case. France can use practically all the grapes she grows, in her own wines; and as these wines can be sold at a very high

profit margin – far higher than the margin on concentrates – it follows that the grapes available for concentrates may well represent the dregs of the crop. The same is not true of countries like Cyprus, Spain, Yugoslavia and even Italy where there are problems of over-production – i.e. they grow far more grapes than can be sold as wine, either at home or abroad. This means that the grapes available for concentrates may represent a very good part of the crop. There is also the question of labour costs. Such costs are high in France and Italy, lower in Spain or Yugoslavia. This again affects the price but not necessarily the quality of the grapes.

Extra concentrate

The standard container of concentrate 'to make a gallon of wine' contains about 27 fluid ounces, or $1\frac{1}{3}$ pints; but, in certain cases, one is offered a jumbo-sized container – also to make a gallon – which contains 40 fluid ounces, or two pints. This extra concentrate is a real benefit, not just because you can cut down on the supplementary sugar, but also because it adds so much more flavour and body to the final wine.

It does seem to me, however, that one is charged rather heavily for this 50% bonus: sometimes as much as a 100% increase on the price of a conventional container. This can be justified in the case of CWE Chianti because they have the added expense of using genuine Tuscany grapes. (I also find the Southern Vinyards Burgundy Superieur is genuinely superior.) But in general, it's as well to keep a wary eye on these de-luxe wine kits. There are more economical ways to add grape sugar, as you will see in Chapter 5.

Special Offers

You will often see that Boots and other winemaking stockists are doing special offers on a particular brand, and the price reduction can be handsome. No need to be suspicious about this because, as with soap powders in a supermarket, the reduction does not reflect any change of quality. It is simply a form of advertising.

Bulk buying

You can also buy larger containers of concentrate which will make up to eight gallons of wine. These can save you around 10% to 20%, but they are not ideal for beginners who are usually well advised to start with smaller quantities. Later on, however, it is a different matter. Some firms will also offer a further discount on large orders collected direct from their premises. (See page 36 for a discussion of where to buy.)

Best Buys

I have collected opinions from many winemakers and retailers; and although there are those who say that – 'they're all much the same, and it doesn't much matter which you buy' – I found that most people had very clear favourites and un-favourites.

CWE have the widest range (at last count, twenty-seven varieties) and they can certainly claim many admirers. They are given a lot of support by the mighty Boots, and their products are easily available in any part of the country. I find their Chianti concentrate is really excellent, and I am also impressed by their vermouth and beaujolais. If you like cream sherries – and, frankly, I don't – the CWE brand is extremely popular. Boots tell me that it out-sells every other variety of grape concentrate. Unican have many friends. Like CWE, the range is wide; and although the price is rather higher, numerous winemakers describe it as excellent value. Another of my own favourites is the Unican burgundy. Garrigos are well spoken of, and I found their rosé very agreeable. Boots have recently begun to put out their own range, and – like most of Boots' own products – these are very reasonably priced and of good quality. The choice is not great, but may be extended in the future.

Perhaps the most enthusiastic comments come from the devotees of Southern Vinyards, and these include the managers of three specialist winemaking stores. (Other satisfied customers include an admiral, a bishop, an air vice-marshal and two members of the peerage – one of whom ordered for many years through his butler.) The Vin Ordinaire, red and white, is reckoned to be unbeatable value, and I have yet to find concentrates that make a better range of white wines. In general, white grape concentrates produce wines that are distinctly darker than their commercial equivalents; and the reason, I am told, is because the grape sugar can get a little burnt during the heat treatment. Southern Vinyards manage to avoid this problem, for their concentrates certainly produce wines of authentic lightness and whiteness.

Future prices
Grape concentrates are zero-rated for British VAT, but other costs –
labour, transport, etc. – are rising steeply. So, also, is the demand for
the juices. Prices are bound to go up; but it is likely that, for some time
to come, the medium-priced brands – like CWE and Garrigos – will remain well under a pound for a gallon of wine. Southern Vinyards Vin
Ordinaire is likely to remain the most economical of all. (Even after a
recent round of price increases, it is currently 57p to make a gallon.)
Another very economical buy is the CWE gallon container of concentrate, to make six gallons of wine, currently priced at £3·02.

Drawbacks
As I said earlier, grape concentrates do have their drawbacks. Sometimes the wine tastes thin and metallic: sometimes they taste extraordinarily alike: (a friend of mine found, in a blind test, that she
couldn't tell a hock from a burgundy!) and invariably, the 'nose' or
bouquet leaves much to be desired. A very experienced winemaker
observed: 'You can't make a really good wine out of a can any more
than you can make a really good soup out of a packet. It's the extras
you add yourself that make all the difference.'
When fresh grapes are out of the question, grape concentrates are undoubtedly the next best thing, and all the recipes in this book will use
them as the main ingredient. But it has been essential to experiment
with many additions, cheap and extravagant, conventional and un-
conventional, to make the results more convincing. Or, in the words
of another friend, to make them – 'more *confusable* with the wines we
know and love'.

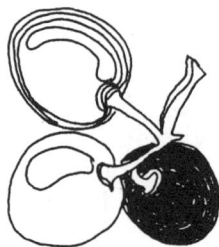

3. Minimum Equipment

Minimum Equipment

By now, you will have some idea of the equipment and ingredients needed for basic winemaking; but, this is only part of the story. In order to make something better than a straight grape concentrate wine, and in order to make the process safer and surer, various extras are needed.

Let me begin, however, by warning you that there is a very dangerous moment in winemaking. It comes before you actually make anything, but you have decided to take the plunge and buy the necessary equipment – and the question arises: '*what is necessary?*' The moment is dangerous because it's so easy to believe that all items on the winemaking shelves are essential. Flushed with a vision of wine at pennies a pint, one feels that almost anything in the way of initial investment is justified.

Advanced winemaking, as you will see, calls for more elaborate equipment; but beginners, who plan to begin with quick-drinking wines based on grape concentrate, need extraordinarily little. A down-to-earth winemaker observed: 'for goodness sake, tell people to save their money for the ingredients' – and this really sums it up. If you're going to spend a little extra on blending and so on, it's all the more important to buy nothing in the way of equipment that is not very necessary indeed.

The following lists will only include the items that I have found indispensable. Some of them, like the plastic bucket or the old Schweppes bottle, you will remember from pages 16–19. Others, like kitchen scales (for weighing out sugar) or a wooden spoon (for stirring things with) are self-explanatory; but you will also see items like pectozyme or yeast nutrient which may not mean much to you. These will all be explained, for if one is to keep one's equipment to a minimum, it is as well to understand the whys and wherefores. Indeed this is so important that I shall not only be giving reasons for putting things in: I shall also be giving reasons for leaving things out.

Hopefully, you will find that most of the real essentials are already living in your kitchen:

Indispensable Equipment

Plastic bucket and cover
Liner for bucket if necessary (see page 17)
Strainer (large and fine-meshed)
Funnel
Wooden spoon
Kitchen scales
Big saucepan (preferably enamel)
8 oz Schweppes screw-top tonic bottle (or something like it)
Disinfectant

This will leave you with the following things to buy:

Glass gallon jars
Flexible tubing for siphoning
Corks
Thermometer (to check on room temperature)

Plus basic ingredients

Concentrate
Wine yeast
Yeast nutrient
Pectozyme

If you have a temperature problem, i.e. a problem in keeping your fermenting wine at the right warmth, you may have to add a special wine heater to your list; but as this difficulty does not affect everyone, I would like to discuss it separately. (See page 30.)
Aside from that, you have everything you need for a six-week wine.

For a longer-maturing wine – one that you plan to keep for three, six or even twelve months – you must add three further items:

Airlocks
Rubber bungs or pierced corks
Campden tablets

Now let's take the items in the lists that need explanation.

Big saucepan. It is sometimes necessary to steep ingredients (like bilberries or wheat) in boiling water so as to extract their sugar and flavour. Sometimes, too, they have to be simmered for short periods on the stove. An enamel saucepan is best because there is less likelihood of the fruit or vegetables picking up any odd metallic flavours.

Disinfectant. This is really self-explanatory, but it's worth emphasising that all winemaking utensils must be kept as clean and sterile as possible. Wine has an ugly habit of picking up bacteria which, at worst, can turn it into irretrievable vinegar. Less disastrously, it will develop strange, unwelcome flavours: these will usually vanish with time, but one would prefer not to have them at all.

Flexible tubing for siphoning. When you transfer wine from one container to another – which is called 'racking' – the main object is to discard the yeasty sludge which has settled at the bottom of the first container. If you tip and pour, it is very difficult to avoid some of the sludge rising in clouds and ending up in the second container. But if you siphon, the original plastic bucket (or jar) will remain upright so the sludge will stay undisturbed at the bottom. A siphon need be nothing more elaborate than a piece of rubber or plastic tubing. You put the full container high up, the empty container low down: then you plunge one end of the tube into the wine, give a good suck at the other end, and direct the flow into the empty container.

Yeast starter bottle. It is perhaps fair to tell you that 'activating' the yeast, as described in basic winemaking, is not always thought to be essential. Many winemakers simply sprinkle the dry wine yeast on a gallon or more of dilute concentrate or juice, and this of course is much easier. It is a fact, however, that the fermentation gets going much more quickly and strongly when activated yeast is used; and as we are aiming to produce wine as fast as possible, a brisk start is important.

Yeast nutrient. This acts on yeast like fertilizer on a plant – i.e. it makes yeast burgeon and blossom. Wine will certainly ferment without its assistance but – as with activated yeast – it is a question of time. Fermentation undoubtedly goes faster when nutrient is used.

Pectozyme. (Sometimes called Pectolytic Enzyme.) This is only necessary when certain fruits and vegetables are included in the recipe – as, for example, peaches, damsons, parsnips, cherries, sloes. These ingredients create a haze in the finished wine; and although this doesn't affect the flavour, the appearance will certainly suffer. The addition of one tablespoonful of pectozyme per gallon will solve the problem; but it must always be remembered that the pectozyme should be put in a) when the liquid is cool, and b) twenty-four hours before the yeast is added.

Airlocks. These are used to seal a jar or cask of fermenting wine. They protect the wines from the outside air; but at the same time, they allow the carbon dioxide gas, generated by the fermentation, to escape. If this gas can't escape, pressure builds up inside the container until the cork blows off or the glass shatters.

Airlocks are not always essential, because wine can ferment quite happily in a covered plastic bucket, or a glass jar plugged with cotton wool. Neither container is sealed tight, so the carbon dioxide gas has an outlet. The danger in this case is that the wine may not be sufficiently protected against the bacteria in the outside air; but, on the other hand, a vigorous fermentation creates a blanket of carbon dioxide which should keep all unwanted germs at bay.

When wine is to be drunk soon after fermentation is over, there is no real necessity for airlocks. They only become desirable when the wine is kept for a longer period and the fermenting gas is no longer active

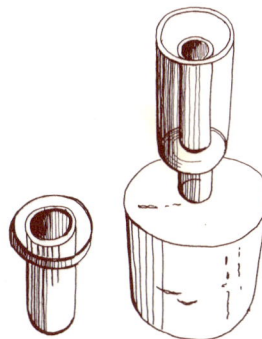

enough to ward off possible bacteria. It then becomes essential to seal the jar, totally, against the outside air; but as there is always a chance of secondary fermentations, it is still wise to allow an outlet for gas.

Bungs. These are really part of the airlocks. They are rubber stoppers – with a hole in the middle: the airlock is fitted into the hole and the stopper is fitted into the neck of the jar. Pierced corks are also used. Airlocks and bungs come in various sizes, depending on the gallonage of your containers; but the principle is always the same. The gas comes out through the hole in the cork and bubbles its strength out in the water contained in the airlock. Many winemakers find this bubbling is a useful guide to the efficiency or otherwise of the fermentation.

Campden tablets. You could call them a disinfectant; and because they have something of a disinfectant flavour they should not be added to quick-drinking wines. These small tablets are usually crushed and added when the fermentation is over, and whenever the wine is subsequently racked. They are extremely good at killing unwanted germs, and are indeed essential for the longer-term vintages (especially the light white wines which are most vulnerable to bacteria). Short term, however, they are undesirable. The quick wines will have been protected for most of their lives by the carbon dioxide, and there is no need for an additional safeguard; and although the Campden flavour will wear off in a month or two, this is not fast enough for wines which may be drunk in a few weeks.

Wine heaters. Many homes will have an airing cupboard, or some place which is consistently warm enough to accommodate the fermenting wine. But if you live in a small flat, or even a bedsitter, you could find there is nothing at all suitable. As temperature is really vital to fermentation – especially when wine is fermented in quantities of one or two gallons – the problem cannot be brushed aside. The only thing to do is invest in a submersible water heater, or an Electrim Fermenter. There are quite a variety of submersible water heaters available now, made specifically for the job of keeping fermenting wine at the ideal temperature. Basically, they are long thin tubes with a built-in electric heater and thermostat. A flex from the top is plugged into an electric point. The tube is then immersed, upright, in the jar or bucket of wine. You are usually able to adjust the temperature so as to make it warmer for red wine (around 75°F) and cooler for white wine (around 68°F). Some of these heaters can cope with five or ten gallons of wine in any container. The Boots brand is made to go in a glass gallon jar and includes a cap, with a hole for the flex, to fit over the top of the jar.

An Electrim Fermenter is more expensive, but it does allow you to ferment several jars of different wine at the same time. This works on a hot-plate principle: you simply stand your jars on the electric heater and switch on. There are no heat controls, but the manufacturers claim that the wine will be kept at a good fermenting temperature. The standard Electrim Fermenter will take two 1-gallon jars, the large one will take four.
Information on where to buy these heaters will be found at the end of the chapter.

Filters
Instructions on the cans of grape concentrate will often urge you to invest in 'wine finings' or filters (to clarify the final wine) but neither of these items are indispensable so far as red wines are concerned. My own experience, and the experience of many other winemakers, is that wines based on red concentrates clear themselves beautifully. Pectozyme may be necessary, and careful racking with a siphon is always desirable, but if these precautions are kept in mind, the wine should be brilliantly clear a few weeks after fermentation.

I must admit, though, that the white wines are a different matter, for although they clear themselves reasonably well, the difference between one that has been filtered and one that has not is quite striking. The trouble is, filters are rather expensive – usually around £3 – and not too easy to handle. Many beginners I spoke to had disliked them very much indeed! On balance, I therefore advise you to forget about them until a later stage and, if necessary, serve your white wines in tinted glasses. (For further information, see page 89.) I have never found that wine finings make more than a marginal difference, so I wouldn't describe them as indispensable even for perfectionists.

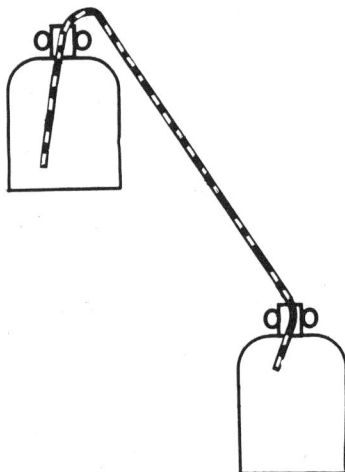

**Siphoning (or Racking)
see page 28**

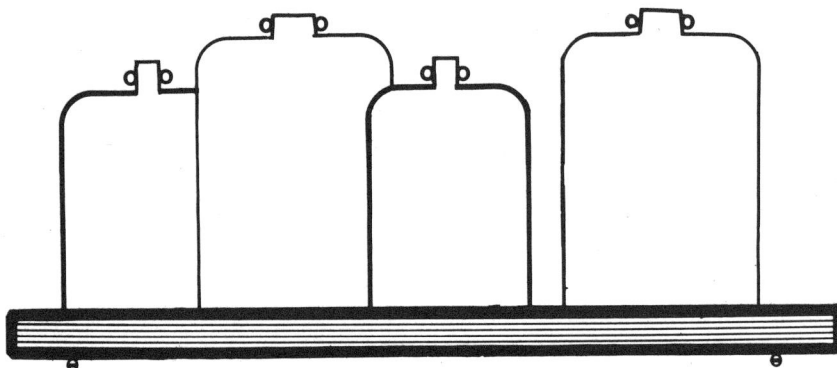

The Electrim Fermenter, see page 31

The hydrometer

There is one further piece of equipment which many experts will tell you is vital – the hydrometer. This is a fairly complicated instrument which gets pages and pages of attention in books on advanced wine-making (often in terms barely comprehensible to beginners). And it is rather comforting to discover how well one's free equipment, eyes and taste, can do its work.

What is a hydrometer? One is usually told that it is an instrument for measuring specific gravity, which is a bad beginning. One may not be quite sure what specific gravity is, and even less sure why one should want to measure it. Specific gravity means, in fact, the density of a liquid; and this density is determined by the amount of sugar the liquid contains. So what it adds up to is something quite simple: the hydrometer tells you how much sugar is present in a liquid. The correct level of sugar, as you will remember from basic winemaking, is crucial; and one can't deny that the hydrometer provides the most accurate method of measurement. When it comes to older and stronger wines, this accuracy becomes essential – (see pages 97–100 on aperitifs and liqueurs) – but short-term table wines are a different matter. You need to know a few elementary facts, but then it is a question of looking and tasting.

Measurement of sugar

This is very simple when wines are based on grape concentrate. A pint of concentrate represents about 1 lb of sugar; so the standard $1\frac{1}{3}$ pint can 'to make a gallon of wine' represents about 1 lb 5 oz. Other ingredients included in the recipes will not make a significant addition because, in order to preserve the main grape flavour, the quantities will be kept very small. You put in the supplementary sugar yourself; and all you have to do is add the amount of supplementary sugar to the amount of grape sugar, and you have, near enough, the total sugar content.

(The sum is not so easy to do when the wine is based on fresh fruit or vegetables or flowers. Their sugar levels vary from place to place and from year to year, and one can't be sure how much is contained in any one pound of parsnips or quart of dandelions. In such cases, the hydrometer comes in useful, but these cases are not being dealt with here.)

You need to know how much sugar will create a dry, medium or sweet wine – and here there is only one fact to be kept in mind. A wine yeast is unlikely to convert to alcohol more than 3 lb sugar per gallon, and anything in excess of this will remain as residual sweetness. The simple rule, therefore, is never to have more than 2½ to 3 lb of sugar per gallon if you want a dry wine. And if you want a medium or sweet wine, you are still well advised to keep to this limit and sweeten to taste *after* the fermentation is over. You can be more exact this way.

Measurement of alcohol strength
Your head will give you some idea of this at a later stage; but you will probably want to choose ahead of time if the wine is to be strong or light or average. Here again, there is only one basic fact to be remembered: a pound of sugar, fermented out, will produce an alcoholic content of approximately 5%. If you have a total of 3 lb sugar in a gallon of liquid, and it ferments out dry, you will have a wine with about 15% alcohol.
With special cossetting, the yeast can do better and the alcoholic content can rise higher. (It is this special cossetting which *does* call for a hydrometer.) But 15% alcoholic content is very strong for a table wine; and many winemakers prefer a total of 2 lb sugar per gallon, and an alcoholic content of 10% or thereabouts – which is what you will find in most commercial table wines.

Checking the fermentation process
This is where the looking and the tasting comes in. Fermentation is a perfectly visible process, with the juice heaving and clouding and bubbling. You can see when it's happening; and as the liquid clears and calms, you can see when it's stopping. You can also taste if the fermentation has 'stuck' – i.e. stopped before the work has been properly done – or has finished correctly, because there is no more sugar available for conversion into alcohol. If the fermentation has stuck, the liquid will taste sweet and you will have to do something about it. (See page 39.) If it tastes dry, you will know that the yeast has performed well and the wine is proceeding to plan. A hydrometer will confirm these findings by registering a large or a small drop in specific gravity; but if you know it already, why bother? A hydrometer will also give you a more accurate assessment of alcoholic content; but it does involve noting the initial and final specific gravities of the juice,

adjusting figures to allow for sugar added during fermentation, adjusting figures to allow for differences in volume, and dividing the answer by 7·36. Most people can't face it.

Bottling
This only deserves a brief mention because it is so evidently a matter of taste and sense. You can keep your wine in a gallon jar, a half-gallon jar, or proper wine bottles, with corks and labels. The expense is small because jars can be used again and again, and it's easy enough to get wine bottles for free. The important thing to remember is that wines, particularly white wines, will go off when they are exposed to the air. (This means you'd have to drink pretty fast if you were pouring direct from a gallon jar.) Remember, too, that the jars or bottles should be kept away from strong light, particularly sunlight. It is safe to use ordinary corks in wine bottles and half-gallon jars, but in case there is slight secondary fermentation, use an airlock in the gallon jar.

Keeping Records
One of the troubles – and fascinations – of winemaking is that no one fermentation seems to come out exactly like another, not even when you use the same ingredients and ferment at the same temperature. (This is why the final blending is so important.) However, you *will* find that certain recipes suit your taste particularly well; and as you progress, you may also find that certain additions or modifications of your own make them turn out even better. For this reason, do try to keep a record of your experiments as this can be very helpful later on – and needn't even be a great chore at the time.

Every time you start off a fermentation, write down the basic details. WINE TYPE, INGREDIENTS, PRICE, DATE. Leave a space for other details which can be filled in as you go along. For example: AMOUNT OF SUGAR ADDED? AT WHAT INTERVALS? HOW OFTEN RACKED? HOW BLENDED?

No need to make hard and fast rules about this. Just write down anything that you think is important and interesting. I myself keep the record sellotaped to the wine container; and when I rack, I simply peel it off and stick it on the next container using, if necessary, another bit of sellotape. When the wine is eventually divided into half gallon jars or bottles, the record goes into my file with a cross reference number. The jars or bottles are labelled with the wine type, date and appropriate number.

Where to Buy

All the basic winemaking equipment and ingredients can usually be found at any large branch of Boots; and other chemists and general stores are beginning to have their winemaking and beer-making counters. However, the recipes will sometimes call for things like dried bilberries or 140° proof Polish spirit, which will probably have to be bought at a specialist winemaking shop. Here, too, you will find a far wider choice of grape concentrates.

There are a fair number of these shops scattered around the country, and one could be close to your home; but if not, your best plan is to take the monthly magazine, *Winemaker*. The advertisements will tell you all about the big stockists, many of whom are willing to send by post anything you care to order. Southern Vinyards for instance operate a special mail order service for customers not within reach of their retail outlets: there are discounts of up to 20% for large orders, plus a further 5% if you can collect yourself from their headquarters in Hove.

Although grape concentrates and yeasts are zero-rated for British VAT, winemaking equipment – regrettably – is not. This is yet another reason for keeping it as minimal as possible.

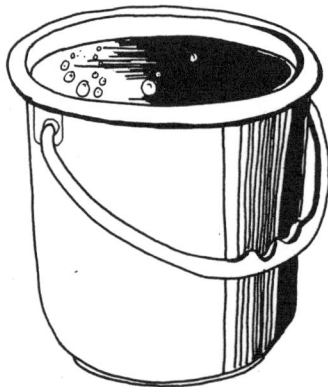

4. Beginners' Bloomers

Beginners' Bloomers

'If people would only read the instructions,' said one winemaker acidly, 'there wouldn't be any bloomers.'

Every can of grape concentrate has on the label – usually the reverse side of the label – simple and exact winemaking instructions; and yet all the grape concentrate firms have told me, with one voice, that a surprising number of people simply fail to read, learn and inwardly digest them. Apparently these firms are always getting furious letters from customers whose wines have refused to ferment; and then inquiries reveal that the customer in question had put the yeast in boiling water, even though blood-heat had been specified: or had put the fermenting jar in a frigid outhouse, even though warned that yeast needed a temperature close to seventy degrees: or indeed had forgotten to put the yeast in at all.

An Oxford don once told me that undergraduates needed to be told a fact four times before they really took it in; so perhaps this is not so surprising. Winemaking is not in the least difficult, but so many people have talked to me about their opening disasters that it seems right to concentrate on the subject for a chapter. I shall at times be saying things that are said in other chapters but, if the Oxford don is right, a little repetition won't hurt. I know my own experiences all went to prove the words of a less acid winemaker who observed, cheerfully:

'When you do something for the first time, or even the first few times, you make the silliest mistakes. I don't know why it should happen to perfectly intelligent people, but it does.'

It's really a question of basic do's and don'ts; and, repetitive though it may be, I'd like to begin with:

Do discover what equipment you really need and don't buy anything else.

As another beginner told me: 'It's so easy to buy everything but the kitchen stove. I bought finings, filters, tannin, maturing agents, claret flavouring, hock flavouring, six different kinds of yeast, acid-reducing compounds – oh yes, and a crown corking gadget. (I didn't realise that was only for beer bottles.)'

It can all add up to a lot of money; and although you may want to experiment with some of these things later on, don't tangle with them at the beginning. Keep to the bare necessities – or, in other words, take another look at the lists in Chapter Three before you go shopping.

And another repetition:
Do activate the yeast before you do anything else.
It often happens that one gets everything ready for the wine, and then remembers that one hasn't done anything about activating the yeast. This isn't a real disaster because the grape concentrate can always wait, or you can sprinkle the yeast on dry; but the first is annoying and the second may get things off to a bad start.

The experts will tell you that a slow, steady fermentation is the best of all; and they will point out that white wines will actually lose flavour and delicacy if they are fermented too fast and furiously. But although this is true, it does not take into account all the realities of the situation. Most beginners will be making wine in small quantities, probably a gallon or two at a time; and one has to face the fact that small quantities of wine do not ferment nearly as well as large. If they start slowly, they will often continue in a sluggish, sulky fashion, perhaps sticking when the juice is still far too sweet.

A brisk fermentation may not be ideal, but it does work. It makes wine fast, it makes wine dry; and any loss of flavour can be compensated by extra ingredients and final blending. However:–

Don't think a stuck fermentation is an Act of God and can't be put right.
You shouldn't have this problem if you activate the yeast and keep the wine at the right temperature. But even when one does everything perfectly, yeast can still misbehave. At times it can seem indestructible – some was discovered, still active, in an ancient Egyptian tomb – yet at others, it will give up for no apparent reason. Many is the beginner who has found his wine stayed syrup – and probably, poured it away.

There's no need for this. The right thing to do is start again, rather as one does with mayonnaise, and see if it cannot be rescued. When mayonnaise curdles, you can make a new lot in another bowl and gradually blend it with the curdled until all has been reclaimed. 'Unsticking' a fermentation follows the same principle.

First you activate a new lot of yeast in the usual starter bottle. After six hours or so, you transfer this to a larger bottle – say an old whisky bottle – and add some of the 'stuck' wine. Don't fill the bottle completely: top it up by degrees, nursing the fermentation along for a day or two. Ideally, you should then transfer to a half-gallon jar and continue the topping up until you can see that the brew is vigorous enough to go in a clean gallon jar with the remainder of the stuck wine. Add some yeast nutrient, and if you do happen to have around another gallon of violently fermenting wine (it needn't be the same type, but it must be the same colour) transfer a pint or so of the active batch to the problem batch – it gives a splendid boost.

Don't think you can get away with the wrong temperature.
You might be able to do so if you were fermenting ten or twenty gallons because, like baker's dough, wine is far better at maintaining and controlling its own temperature when made in bulk. But a gallon or so won't have a chance.
Yeast strains vary and you can't know for sure when the heat will kill it or the cold will paralyse it. But it's safe to say that any temperature over eighty or under fifty degrees Fahrenheit is dangerous; and any temperature other than those between sixty-five and seventy-five degrees is risky. The ideal for white wine is rather under seventy, and the ideal for red rather over that; and, ideally again, the warmth should be steady and consistent in a draught-free place like an airing cupboard.

Don't start off with too much sugar – even if you want a sweet wine.
Yeast can't cope with too much sugar at once: this is why gradual sugar feeding is recommended when one is making stronger wines, like port, which involve trying to get the yeast to convert as much sugar as possible into alcohol. As a safe and general rule, you can say that each gallon of liquid should start fermenting with a sugar content not in excess of 2½ lb. Not more than 8 oz sugar should be added during fermentation. The wine should end up dry; but it can be sweetened to taste at a later stage.

The facts about the Vinegar Fly and bacteria.
Winemaking books all emphasise the importance of strict hygiene and, although one might like to think that they make too much of a fuss

about it, the dangers of non-hygiene are incontrovertible. Vinegar flies are anxious to get into the wine; and if they succeed, they will turn it to vinegar. Wine is very ready to pick up germs and flavours from dirty utensils and containers; and it will also pick up strains of wild yeast from the air or from tap water, and such strains can affect the taste disagreeably.

However it seems to me that commonsense hygiene is all that is really required; and it shouldn't be necessary to use nothing but boiled water, to go in for steam heat sterilization, to mix up special sterilizing solutions (like sodium metabisulphate and citric acid) and to go more or less mad every time a fly comes in sight. One is even told that, as vinegar flies can leave their contamination in the air, one must protect wine from the air *where they might have been.* And to me, this is rather like being told that one must never get between a mamba snake and its hole: how can you know where the hole *is*?

The common sense precautions are as follows:

1) All containers and utensils must be thoroughly washed and sterilized before use, but you needn't mix up anything special. An ordinary disinfectant like Domestos or Jeyes Fluid will do.

2) You must rinse well with water *after* using the disinfectant because yeast dislikes fermenting in disinfectant fumes. Also they might leave some of their own (unlovable) flavour in the wine.

3) There is a chance of picking up bacteria and wild yeast from ordinary tap water; and if you have doubts about the hygiene of your own supply, it might be wise to use boiled water – both for rinsing utensils and for making the wine. In general, though, the risk is fairly remote.

4) Wine becomes more vulnerable to infection once the fermentation, with its protective blanket of carbon dioxide, is over. (Vinegar flies don't have a chance when faced with carbon dioxide.) Fermented wine must, therefore, be allowed as little contact with the air as possible; and this is the reason for keeping jars and bottles both full and stoppered. (Use cotton

wool for short-term fermentation, airlocks or corks for long-term operations).

5) Sugar and alcohol act as a guard against germs, so sweet and fortified wines are less at risk. Use extra care with dry table wines, particularly those with a low alcoholic content.

The final 'don't' sounds rather terrible, but it has to be said:

Don't let the first taste of your wine fill you with total despair.
Everything may have been done right, the fermentation may have gone like a breeze, but you may still think that you have never tasted anything so horrible in all your life.
This is the moment to remember that young wines in a French vineyard can taste equally appalling. But if you are hoping to drink the wine soon, and not allow the mellowing years to do their work, it is even more important to realise that some swift rescue work *can* be done to give the wine the flavour, the body, the smoothness which it is so evidently lacking. This is the subject of the next chapter.

5. How to Make and Blend your Daily Wine

How to Make and Blend your Daily Wine

The importance of Vin Ordinaire looms large in the lives of many people today, because the habit of taking wine with meals has become such a regular one. Unless you're astonishingly rich, your regular glass cannot be filled with anything very old or very grand: to borrow some of the familiar phrases, it has to be 'an unpretentious little character' with 'adequate body' and 'agreeable vinosity'. In other words, it has to be a good daily wine.

By and large, this is the wine that people are most anxious to make for themselves; and it's lucky that it happens to be the quickest and easiest wine to make – indeed, the obvious way to begin a winemaking life. I have found there are three ways to make a rapid and drinkable Vin Ordinaire:

1) Using extra grape concentrate and bananas.

2) Blending with an extra sweet, extra fruity wine which you have made yourself.

3) Blending with commercial wines – usually fortified wines like port, sherry or Dubonnet.

In Chapter Seven I shall be describing a different and rather more expensive form of blending, designed to make your Vin distinctly less Ordinaire; but for the moment we are dealing with daily wines which, because they *are* daily, must be kept as economical as possible.

The basic principle behind these three methods is the same; and it is that wine, if it is to be made quicker must be made stronger – slightly stronger in alcohol, definitely stronger in flavour. In this respect, it's rather like making instant coffee as opposed to fresh coffee from freshly-roasted and ground coffee beans: the second variety involves more time and trouble, but it produces something with a far more delectable aroma and flavour, and it doesn't need to be strong in order to be good. Instant coffee has a far straighter, less subtle flavour, and if it is made weak and watery, the taste can be very dim indeed. Make it stronger and it begins to improve: it's still not as good as the fresh coffee, but at least there is a coffee flavour.

The finest wine flavours and bouquets come from a slow chemical reaction between the various elements in the grape. This can take years to develop fully, and there is no known way to hurry it along. Young wines cannot possibly belong in the same category, and indeed, the young grape flavour tends to be rather disagreeable. Like instant coffee, it has no delicious overtones or subtleties; and when it is weak, it is also thin and sharp. When, however, it is stronger it begins to get fullness and roundness. What is more important, it begins to taste like wine.

Extra grape concentrate and extra sugar are a great help. So – rather unexpectedly – are bananas. This fruit has a bland, unobtrusive taste which will not interfere with the main grape flavour; but it adds immediate body and smoothness to a wine, taking the edge off the young sharpness. As an added advantage, the banana is almost as good as the grape at producing clear, bright wines.

The use of honey instead of sugar has an excellent 'smoothing' effect on wine; but unluckily, the price of honey is a bit dismaying – almost six times the price of ordinary granulated sugar. Try it once to see if you think the difference is worth the extra money; and if you decide it is, look around for ways of buying honey more cheaply in bulk. (You can knock at least 25% off the price this way.)

The first recipe for Vin Ordinaire is designed to be drunk on its own, without the help of blending with other wines. It will make use of all the extras: extra grape concentrate, extra sugar and a bonus of bananas. The alcoholic content will be higher than that of most commercial wines, so you should drink it with respect, or perhaps with the addition of a little water.

Daily Wine 1

This can be red, white or rosé, according to your preference; and you can also choose the wine type that appeals to you most – burgundy, beaujolais, hock, chablis and so on and so forth. My own preference is for the CWE beaujolais, the Unican rosé, and the Southern Vinyards champagne – which, as well as making champagne, makes a good straight wine of a really light colour.

For two gallons, buy two cans of your chosen type; and, at the same time, buy a can of straight red or white concentrate. Boots own brand is the most economical. (Use a white for the rosé.)
Other ingredients will be:

    wine yeast (2 teasp.)
    wine nutrient (1 teasp.)
    2 lb granulated sugar
    (or 8 oz sugar and 2 lb honey)
    1 lb bananas

You now follow the procedure outlined in basic winemaking (page 18), but with a few additions.

1   Activate the yeast – i.e. fill an 8 oz Schweppes tonic bottle half-full of blood-heat water, add two rounded teaspoonfuls of wine yeast, shake well, and leave in a warm place (close to 70°F) for six hours.

2   Peel and slice one banana, cover with boiling water, and leave for about the same length of time as the yeast.

3   Leave the cans of grape concentrate in a warm place for a few hours; or, alternatively, stand them in very hot water for about thirty minutes. In cold conditions, the juice can crystallise and be rather awkward to pour out; but once warmed, the juice runs easily.

4   Pour the concentrate into a plastic bucket. Rinse the cans thoroughly, and add this water, too. Strain the liquid from the bananas; then make up the total liquid to two gallons with blood-heat water.

5   Add 1 lb sugar (or 1 lb honey) and stir thoroughly.

6   Add yeast, cover the bucket with lid, foil or cloth, and leave in a warm place for three days.

7   Dissolve 1 lb sugar (or 1 lb honey and 8 oz sugar) in a little warm water and stir into the bucket. Add a teaspoonful of yeast nutrient.

8   Leave for a week. By this time all signs of the fermentation, which may have been violent on occasions, should have subsided. The yeast particles will be sinking to the bottom, and the liquid clearing. The taste should be fairly dry.

9   Siphon the wine equally into two glass gallon jars. It will be necessary to top up both with cold water.

10   Plug the jars with cotton wool and leave at room temperature for three or four weeks. Fermentation will continue, gently, during this period; and wine will become even dryer.

11   Siphon the wine into glass jars or bottles, ready for drinking. It may be a little fizzy but this will disappear if, a few hours before use, you pour into a decanter and leave open.

If you read the instructions on the various cans of grape concentrate, you will see that there are other, slightly different procedures in winemaking mainly involving making smaller quantities. They all work well, but I prefer the method I've described for the following reasons:

First – the extra grape concentrate means an extra-violent fermentation. This doesn't matter in a plastic bucket, where there is room for activity, but you can run into trouble when you are told to ferment in a glass gallon jar with an airlock. The juice can keep rising and over-flowing through the airlock and pouring, most messily, down the sides of the jar. A lot of mopping up is involved.

Second – a lot of sludge is left at the end of every fermentation, and buckets are easier to clean than jars: you can really get down to the bottom. The one possible drawback to plastic containers has already been discussed (see page 17) but so long as you use white plastic, there should be no danger. The use of transparent polythene bags to line the bucket or bin is a small added expense, but it does guarantee absolute cleanliness and sterility. These bags can, of course, only be used once.

Third – you can make more than a gallon at a time. It can be a little awkward to make a gallon, using 50% extra concentrate, because you may be left with half a can of juice. (You can, of course, use the 'jumbo' cans discussed in Chapter Two, but they work out more expensive.) Also, it does help the fermentation if you make a larger quantity; and if the space is available, I would recommend four or five gallons in a plastic dustbin rather than one or two in a bucket. It's hardly more trouble, the results are better, and you won't have to make wine again so soon.

There may, however, be those who only want to make a gallon at a time. This could be for reasons of space, or you could – very sensibly – feel that you don't want to make too much of any one wine until you're sure you like it. You might also want to experiment with several different wine types, and this is easier done in small rather than large amounts.

In this case, Daily Wine 2 (page 51) or Daily Wine 3 (page 53) may suit you better. No extra grape concentrate with extra-violent fermen-tation is involved, and it is perfectly easy to use a glass gallon jar with an airlock. As you will see, this means very little difference in the procedure. Both these recipes are based on blending, either with your own or with commercial wines; and as this is a big subject, let's begin with a summary of the general blending principles.

Blending Principles

It's better to begin with a *dry* wine; and, as has been said before, this remains true even when you want a sweet, or very sweet wine. Blending in sweetness and body is far easier than blending away a syrupy flavour; and you don't have to worry if the wine is thin and sharp as well as dry. The correct blending will soon put this right.

Don't *entirely* trust your own taste. Blending to taste sounds easy, but there are pitfalls. It's extraordinary how different a wine can taste at different times of day, and how something that seemed nice and smooth at eleven o'clock in the morning may strike you as far too sweet and fruity at lunch: or how the taste that seemed rough around tea time can turn out ideal with the dinner steak.
The safest thing for a beginner to do is keep a commercial Vin Ordinaire to hand, one that you have been buying and liking for some time. As you blend, keep tasting the bought wine and using it as a yardstick, and this way you should come out right.

Basic blending is *not* a question of adding like to like; and you would get poor results if you simply added a bought burgundy to a homemade burgundy. Like to like can be done at a later stage (see Chapter Seven) – but at the moment, the object is to give flavour, smoothness and body to a thin young wine. To do this economically, you need to blend with a wine that is the opposite: i.e. very sweet, very smooth, very fruity. This is why fortified wines, like port, sherry and Dubonnet are so good.

Don't be afraid to experiment – for this is part of the fun. I tried a mixture of ordinary white wine with dry vermouth (both homemade) and found that it tasted like the Greek wine, retsina. This was quite unexpected, and all the more enjoyable for that reason. Good cooks don't stick forever to book recipes, and neither do good winemakers.
If you plan to make a wine that can be offered, confidently, to other people, you must continue to be suspicious of your own taste. You yourself, dabbling in a home cellar, may get used to flavours that would strike anyone else as odd and un-wine-like; and this is where a little help from one's friends can come in very helpful indeed.

I have found that the best tests are blind. If you hand someone a glass with the winning inquiry – 'What do you think of my homemade burgundy?' – reactions are likely to be confused. They may not want to hurt your feelings, or they may find it impossible to believe that homemade burgundy is anything but vile; and what they actually *say* could be an unconstructive mixture of politeness and prejudice.

If, however, you line up three glasses and tell your friend: 'These glasses contain two commercial burgundies, one contains the home-made brand – now tell me which is which?' Well, the verdict will at least be objective. It is a real triumph if the homemade burgundy is rated commercial; and if your own burgundy was, unerringly, dubbed home-made, you can at least learn why. Was it the colour? the bouquet? different flavour? in what way 'different'? Hopefully the difference, if pinpointed, can be put right.

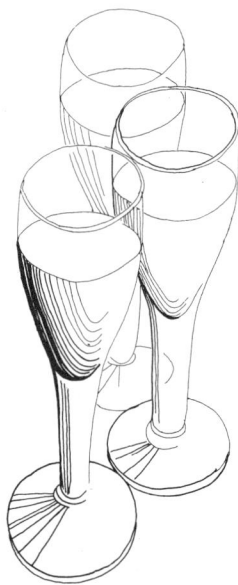

Daily Wine 2

You begin, in the same way, by settling on a wine colour and a wine type; but this time you only buy a single can of concentrate, and this time you ferment in a glass gallon jar with no extras. Ingredients will simply be:

> 1 can grape concentrate (red, white or rosé)
> 12 oz sugar (or 1 lb honey)
> wine yeast (2 teasp.)
> yeast nutrient (1 teasp.)

The method is as follows:–

1. Activate the yeast (page 18).

2. Warm the can of concentrate.

3. Pour the concentrate into the jar, rinse the can thoroughly and add this water to the jar.

4. Dissolve 6 oz sugar in warm water and add to the jar. Make up to 7 pints of liquid (about 7/8 full) with blood-heat water.

5. Add the yeast, fit airlock (page 29) and leave in a warm place for five days.

6. Dissolve 6 oz sugar in warm water and add to the jar together with 1 teasp. yeast nutrient.

7. Top up the jar with water, replace the airlock and leave for three weeks.

8. Siphon the wine into clean gallon jar, topping up with water where necessary. Plug with cotton wool.

9. Leave in a cooler place for about a week, after which the wine will be ready for blending.

The blending operation

For red wine, use a ruby port (Sandeman's is good) or Dubonnet. Use a white port or a good cream sherry for the white wine. (The sherry has a slight colour disadvantage, but you won't be using enough of it for this to make a real difference.) A really fruity hock blends well with the rosé, with perhaps a little tawny port.

Pour $\frac{1}{4}$ pint of your own wine into a mug; and alongside, put a wine-glassful of the blending wine. As mentioned earlier, it is a great help if you can also have available a commercial wine of the same type to act as a yardstick.

Add a few drops of the blending wine to your own, and taste. Another few drops, another taste. Continue until you feel the sweetness and smoothness is right.

You will now be able to assess how much of the blending wine is needed for each pint of your own wine. Tastes vary; but I find, on average, that about $\frac{1}{3}$ bottle of port, Dubonnet or sherry is needed for each gallon of homemade wine, and about a bottle of hock for the rosé.

The wine may now be bottled (see page 35). I usually blend two pints at a time in a large jug and pour into wine bottles, or, even simpler, into $\frac{1}{2}$ gallon jars. Keep tasting, each time you blend, to make sure you find it right. If, in retrospect, you think you have over-sweetened, sharpen up the taste with a little very dry sherry or Noilly Prat.

Daily Wine 3

You begin, as with Daily Wine 2 (page 51), by making a gallon of red, white or rosé; but this time you blend with your own wine. This method takes more time and trouble than blending with commercial wines; but it does, of course, work out very much cheaper.

The trick is to make a wine, red or white, which is deliberately over-sweet and over-fruity. You ought to keep it for at least six months to allow the flavour to develop, and unless you have a sweet wine tooth, you probably won't want to drink it on its own. But it should be excellent for blending with brand new vintages.

Red Blending Wine

2 cans red grape concentrate (like Boots own brand)
2 lbs bananas
2 lbs fresh grapes
½ pint of red rose petals (if available)
wine yeast
yeast nutrient
2 Campden tablets
1 lb honey

1. Activate the yeast (page 18).
2. Peel and slice the bananas, put in a plastic bucket and cover with boiling water.
3. Add grape concentrate to the bucket, stirring well.
4. Put the grapes into a clean nylon stocking – about ¼ lb at a time – and squeeze out the juice with your hands into a jug or bowl. Add this juice to the bucket.
5. Make up to about nine pints of lukewarm liquid, add yeast, cover the bucket and put in a warm place. Leave for three days.

6. Add the rose petals to the bucket. Leave for two days, stirring daily.
7. Add the honey, dissolved in warm water, together with a teaspoonful of yeast nutrient. Leave for four days, stirring daily.
8. Strain the liquid into a second bucket. Leave at room temperature for two days for sediment to settle, then siphon into a gallon jar.
9. Add two crushed Campden tablets, fit an airlock and leave at room temperature for three months.
10. Siphon into a clean gallon jar, topping up with water, and leave for three months with an airlock.

The wine should now be ready for blending use; but you will probably find that it needs some final sweetening – up to 1 lb sugar in the gallon.

White Blending Wine

2 cans white grape concentrate
2 lbs bananas
2 lbs fresh grapes
4 oz mixed dried fruit
$\frac{1}{4}$ pint fresh elderflowers (if available)
wine yeast
yeast nutrient
2 Campden tablets
1 lb honey

The procedure is exactly the same as for the red blending wine. The mixed dried fruit should be put in with the bananas and covered with boiling water; and the fresh elderflowers should be added at the same time as the rose petals. (If elderflowers are not available, white rose petals will do.)
This white wine can also be used for blending with rosé.

6. How to Make Burgundy, Beaujolais, Chianti, Hock, Moselle, Champagne, and other Regional Wines

How to Make Burgundy, Beaujolais, Chianti, Hock, Moselle, Chablis, Champagne and other Regional Wines

The wines described here *can* be drunk in six weeks, especially if you follow the blending routine suggested in the next chapter. But the wine certainly develops a better flavour – more hock-like, more burgundy-like and so on – if it is allowed to mature for a few months after fermentation is over. Waiting isn't so hard when you have abundant and rapid supplies of daily wine to hand; so at least hold back a few bottles and see for yourself what the difference in taste can be.

The wine that needs longest of all is claret; and I'm afraid one cannot pretend that anything authentic will emerge in six or even twelve months. The full claret flavour develops from grapes with a high tannin content, and this tannin begins by tasting very harsh. It is, literally, a matter of years before the chemical processes in a maturing wine can break it down into something smooth and beautiful. The claret recipe given here is the best one can do, short term; but the real claret lover should look ahead to Chapter Ten to see what, realistically, a wine like this involves.

The basis of all these recipes is grape concentrate, but most wine-makers, myself included, find that the addition of certain other ingredients *in small quantities* will not only help with the body, bouquet and colour: they will also help the right flavour to emerge.

I keep emphasising 'small quantities' because it is all too easy to overdo these other ingredients; and when this happens, their own flavour begins to take over from the grape and the wrong taste emerges. Two ingredients, much recommended in winemaking recipes, are good cases in point: raisins (or sultanas) and elderberries.

Rasins and sultanas have every advantage except one. They're economical, they help fermentation, they add a splendid amount of body, but – although they started life as grapes – they have a flavour all their own which is nothing like the grape. This flavour, rather prune-y and scented, is extremely pervasive; and even in small quantities, I find that dried fruits are risky ingredients.

The same is true of elderberries. The flavour is strong and distinctive, very liable to swamp the grape and turn the wine into a good old-fashioned elderberry wine. However, I have found that in really small quantities they can be excellent for they add the touch of astringency that one associates with wines like chianti. They also impart the most beautiful colour to a wine, brilliantly rich and red.

Elderflowers and rose petals, if used with caution, can be invaluable for they add the thing that is most noticeably lacking from grape concentrates – bouquet. There is a danger that both taste and bouquet could be a little over-scented, over-flower-like; but as flowers are much less strongly flavoured than fruits, the risk is not great. You will see that most recipes include these ingredients, but of course, they may not always be available. If this is the case, I'm afraid there is no real alternative: dried elderflowers or rose petals can be used, but I find them rather musty and unsatisfactory.

In general, there is a wide range of ingredients which aid and abet the main grape flavour. Some of these, like fresh peaches or sloes, are not available all the year round, and this is one reason why I am giving two recipes for each wine type, so that there will always be an alternative. Another reason may be on grounds of economy: one recipe could be more extravagant than the other.

Finally, a word about supplementary sugar. There are alternatives to ordinary granulated sugar – invert sugar, honey, demerara sugar, raw Barbados sugar, golden syrup, even black treacle – and you may want to know about their pros and cons.

Invert sugar is sugar that has been split into two component parts – glucose and fructose; and this splitting operation has to be performed before alcohol can be produced. When ordinary granulated sugar is added, the yeast must first 'invert' it into glucose and fructose; but if the sugar has already been inverted, the yeast can get straight on with the business of conversion to alcohol. It follows, therefore, that invert sugar helps fermentation because it saves the yeast both time and work.

Invert sugar can be bought direct, or you can make it yourself (see page 100–1). I have not found it necessary for table wines as activated yeast seems perfectly capable of coping with limited amounts of the granulated variety. One must remember, too, that grape sugar is naturally inverted, so the yeast will have no extra work to do there. When one is trying to get the maximum alcohol, invert sugar becomes much more desirable; and as you will see, it is recommended for stronger wines.

Honey, like grape sugar, is a natural invert, and has everything except price to recommend it. Scientific winemakers wax eloquent about the beneficial effects of its pollen grains, floral esters and trace elements; and it certainly seems to produce a much smoother, more delicately flavoured wine. It is not so important for the heavier wines, like burgundy or sauternes, but the lighter beaujolais, chablis, moselle and so on benefit enormously. These wines do not have a lot of body and there is always a danger that they will taste thin. Honey, with its smoothing influence, can turn thinness into lightness – a vital difference. The following recipes will usually recommend that at least part of the supplementary sugar is added in the form of honey, but granulated sugar can always be substitued if you find this too expensive. *Remember that 1 lb of honey equals only 12 oz sugar,* so if you are exchanging one for the other, the quantities must always be adjusted. And one final point: be careful to use the right colour of honey. Obviously, a dark honey is unsuitable for a white wine.

Demerara sugar is perfectly suitable for all red wines – not so good for white because of the colour – but I have not found that it makes a very noticeable difference one way or the other. Raw Barbados sugar, golden syrup, black treacle are all too strongly flavoured to be really suitable; and for white wines, the colour problem is even worse than with demerara sugar. Try them by all means if you like to experiment; but I myself always stay with granulated sugar, honey and invert sugar for stronger wines.

Most recipes recommend a final sweetening to taste with sugar or glycerine when the fermentation is over and the wine has been racked once or twice. This is perfectly all right, but results are undeniably better for the flavour when the final sweetening is done with grape juice. A rather heavy sweet variety made by Epicure is ideal.

Beaujolais 1

1 can Beaujolais Grape Concentrate
(to make a gallon of wine)
1 oz dried bilberries
½ lb fresh grapes
¼ pint red rose petals
12 oz sugar, or 1 lb honey
wine yeast
yeast nutrient
1 Campden tablet

Activate the yeast.

Put the grape concentrate and the bilberries in a plastic bucket together with the juice squeezed from the fresh grapes through a nylon stocking. Cover with hot water and stir well.

Make up to a gallon of lukewarm liquid and add yeast. Cover the bucket and leave in a warm place (70°F to 75°F) for three days.

Dissolve the honey or sugar in warm water and add to the bucket together with 1 teaspoonful of nutrient and freshly-picked rose petals. Leave for five days.

Strain the liquid into a second plastic bucket and leave at room temperature for two days, allowing the sediment to settle.

Siphon the liquid into a gallon jar, add a crushed Campden tablet, fit an airlock and leave for three months. The jar can be left at room temperature (or cooler).

Rack again into clean jars or bottles.

The wine may be drunk after a few days, but will improve considerably if it is kept a further three months and racked a second time.

☐ *Beaujolais is a light red wine, quite smooth, but without any pungent flavour. It's the kind that most drinkers put away happily and rather unnoticingly; and you may well find that it is one of your safest offerings. Even when made in France, beaujolais is drunk young, so no one should expect anything very mature or subtle in the way of taste.*

Beaujolais 2

1 can Beaujolais Grape Concentrate
2 oz dried bilberries
2 bananas
1 lemon
$\frac{1}{4}$ pint rose petals
12 oz sugar or 1 lb honey
wine yeast
yeast nutrient
1 Campden tablet

Activate yeast.
Put grape concentrate, bilberries and sliced bananas in plastic bucket and cover with boiling water. Stir well, and leave until cool.
Add juice of lemon, and make up to a gallon of lukewarm liquid.
Proceed as in Beaujolais 1 (page 59).

□ *This recipe will produce a wine with more body.*

Burgundy 1

2 cans Burgundy Concentrate
(rather extravagant for 1 gallon of wine, but the results are good)
7 oz canned red cherries
$\frac{1}{2}$ pint red rose petals
8 oz sugar
wine yeast
yeast nutrient
pectozyme (1 tablespoonful)
1 Campden tablet

Activate yeast.
Put cherries and juice in saucepan, cover with boiling water and leave until cool.
Stir in pectozyme and leave twenty-four hours.
Put grape concentrate in bucket, strain on liquid from cherries and proceed as in Beaujolais 1 (page 59).

☐ *Burgundy is a heavier, stronger wine – more suitable for dinner than for lunch. Again, it is a type that drinkers are very familiar with, and that they will not – probably – be over-critical about. Be careful to serve at a warm room temperature as anything colder will make it taste raw.*

Burgundy 2

1 can Burgundy Grape Concentrate
1 oz dried elderberries
3 bananas
½ pint red rose petals
1½ lbs sugar
wine yeast
yeast nutrient
1 Campden tablet

Activate the yeast.
Put the elderberries and sliced bananas in a bucket, cover with boiling water, stir in 1 lb sugar, and leave until lukewarm.
Stir in the grape concentrate and proceed as for Beaujolais 1 (page 59).

☐*A lighter, less extravagant version of Burgundy 1 with a slightly more astringent flavour.*

Claret 1

1 can Claret Grape Concentrate
1 lb fresh damsons or sloes
2 bananas
4 oz sugar
1 lb honey
$\frac{1}{4}$ pint red rose petals
wine yeast
yeast nutrient
pectozyme (1 tablespoonful)
2 Campden tablets

Activate the yeast.
Remove the stones from the sloes or damsons, mash them with a fork and put in saucepan together with the sliced bananas and sugar. Cover with boiling water and leave until cool.
Stir in the pectozyme and leave for 24 hours.
Put the concentrate in a bucket, strain on the liquid from the saucepan and proceed as in Beaujolais 1 (page 59).

☐ *It has already been admitted that one cannot get really close, short term, to the connoisseur's wine. At worst, however, your friends will think it is a rather astringent beaujolais, which is quite enjoyable. And if you get the temperature right, the thought of claret should certainly come to mind. Fresh damsons or sloes, with their tannin content, give the best results, but if these are not available, try Claret 2.*

Claret 2

1 can Claret Grape Concentrate
1 lb fresh grapes
2 bananas
¼ pint elderflowers
4 oz sugar
1 lb honey
wine yeast
yeast nutrient
2 Campden tablets

Activate the yeast.
Slice the bananas, put in a bucket and cover with boiling water. Stir in the sugar and grape concentrate.
Add the squeezed grape juice to the bucket.
Mix the remaining grape pulp in boiling water and add to the bucket.
Make up to a lukewarm gallon of liquid and proceed as in Beaujolais 1 (page 59).

Chianti 1

1 can Chianti Concentrate
(The CWE one has 50% extra grape concentrate)
1 oz dried elderberries
1 tablespoonful Ribena or other blackcurrant syrup
2 lemons
2 bananas
12 oz sugar
yeast nutrient
wine yeast
2 Campden tablets

Activate the yeast.
Put the elderberries, Ribena, sliced bananas and thinly pared rind of lemon in a bucket together with the grape concentrate. Cover with boiling water, stir well and leave until cool.
Add the juice of the two lemons and make up to a gallon with warm water.
Proceed as on page 59, except that the sugar should be added in two stages: 6 oz with a ½ teaspoonful of nutrient after three days, 6 oz with ½ teaspoonful of nutrient after a further three days.
The liquid should be siphoned into a gallon jar four days after the last dose of sugar.

☐*The traditional chianti, made in Tuscany, is on the rugged side and many drinkers find it an acquired taste. You must certainly try it if you are fond of pasta – they make a splendid combination – and as I mentioned earlier, this is one of the rare cases where the right grapes are available in concentrated form. Italian peasants will also add stalks and pips and leaves and even twigs to give "bite"; and although the CWE Chianti Concentrate is excellent, extra ingredients are needed to give the requisite roughness.*

Chianti 2

1 can Chianti Concentrate
2 oz dried bilberries
1 lemon
½ pint red rose petals
1 lb honey
yeast nutrient
wine yeast
2 Campden tablets

Put the bilberries in a saucepan, cover with boiling water and leave until cool.
Put the grape concentrate and the juice of lemon in a bucket, strain on the liquid from saucepan and make up to a gallon with warm water.
Proceed as in Beaujolais 1 (page 59).

☐ *This is smoother in taste and not as high in alcohol.*

Rosé 1

1 can Rosé Concentrate
7 oz green gooseberries (canned)
½ pint Schloer Apple Juice
¼ pint elderflowers
12 oz sugar
yeast nutrient
wine yeast
2 Campden tablets
pectozyme

Activate the yeast.
Mash up the gooseberries in a saucepan with about a tablespoonful of juice. Add a tablespoonful of pectozyme, cover with cold water and leave for forty-eight hours.
Put the grape concentrate in a bucket, strain on liquid from the gooseberries, and make up to a gallon with warm water.
Stir in 6 oz sugar, add the yeast and proceed as on page 59. Add apple juice towards the end of the fermentation.

When in season, use fresh peaches rather than canned gooseberries. You will need four large peaches, or six smaller ones. Mash them up in a saucepan, removing the stones, and cover with boiling water. When cool, add a tablespoonful of pectozyme and leave for forty-eight hours. Add the strained liquid to the grape concentrate in a bucket.

☐*Like beaujolais, this wine is very easy to accept. It can go with almost anything in the way of food; and is pleasant to drink, iced, as a summer aperitif. You will probably find that it is drunk, uncritically, in rather large quantities; but as it is not too alcoholic, this won't do any harm.*

Rosé 2

Make a gallon of rosé as in the previous recipe but when you rack the second time, siphon wine into champagne bottles.

Activate some yeast (preferably champagne yeast) in the usual way.

Put the sugar in bowl, allowing 1 level teaspoonful for every bottle, and mix in enough activated yeast to form a solution.

Divide this solution equally among your champagne bottles, topping up each in turn. Be careful not to fill them right to the top as an inch or two of air space is needed.

Cork with a long champagne-type cork and wire down securely. (A corking kit is available at specialist wine stores.)

Leave bottles in cool place for at least a month.

(You can chance your arm and use ordinary screw-top bottles, like cider or beer bottles. This makes it all much easier, but the sparkling wine can sometimes burst the glass. Also, it doesn't look so chic to pour sparkling rosé, still less champagne, out of an old beer bottle.)

Other ways to add sparkle will be discussed in the champagne recipes. (See page 83.)

☐*Sparkling rosé, Portuguese style, is very popular these days; and although it calls for some extra equipment and extra work, you may find that both are worth while.*

Hock 1

1 can Hock Concentrate
2 lbs good quality white grapes
7 oz gooseberries (canned)
1 pint apple juice (Schloer or St Michael from Marks & Spencer
  is best)
¼ pint white or yellow rose petals
1 lb honey
yeast nutrient
wine yeast
2 Campden tablets
pectozyme

Mash the gooseberries in a tablespoonful of juice, add a tablespoonful of pectozyme and leave to soak in a quart of cold water for forty-eight hours.
Put grape concentrate in bucket together with juice squeezed from fresh grapes through a nylon stocking.
Strain liquid from gooseberries into bucket, make up to a gallon with warm water, add yeast and proceed as on page 59. Apple juice should be added with the rose petals.

☐*In general I have found the hock concentrates very thin and un-fruity – not at all reminiscent of Germany. It has been necessary to be a little extravagant in some of the extra ingredients; but hock, if it is to deserve the name, must have a certain fullness and ripeness of flavour.*

Hock 2

1 can Hock Concentrate
1 lb white grapes
7 oz rhubarb (canned)
2 large fresh peaches
$\frac{1}{2}$ pint apple juice
$\frac{1}{4}$ pint white or yellow rose petals
1 lb honey
yeast nutrient
wine yeast
2 Campden tablets
pectozyme

Mash the rhubarb and stoned peaches together, add a tablespoonful of pectozyme and leave to soak in a quart of cold water for forty-eight hours.
Proceed as in Hock 1 (page 69).
If fresh peaches are not available, use 4 oz canned gooseberries.

☐*Not quite so full and fruity.*

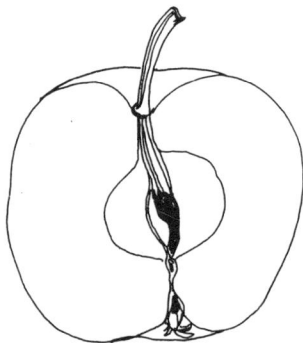

Moselle 1

1 can Moselle Concentrate
7 oz lychees (canned)*
1 lemon
$\frac{1}{4}$ pint elderflowers
1 lb honey
yeast nutrient
wine yeast
2 Campden tablets
pectozyme

Mash the lychees and put in a saucepan together with the thinly pared rind of the lemon. Add tablespoonful of pectozyme and soak in a quart of cold water for forty-eight hours.

Put the concentrate in a bucket with the juice from the lemon, strain on liquid from the lychees and lemon rind and proceed as in Beaujolais 1 (page 59).

*If fresh lychees are available, so much the better. Use 6 oz – weighed *after* they have been peeled and stoned.

☐*This, in some contrast to hock, is a crisp light wine, not heavy on flavour. Always serve well chilled; and you will find that few things taste nicer on a summer's day with a plateful of strawberries and cream.*

Moselle 2

1 can Moselle Concentrate
4 oz sugar
1 orange
$\frac{1}{4}$ pint elderflowers
$\frac{1}{2}$ pint grape juice (white)
1 lb honey
yeast nutrient
wine yeast
2 Campden tablets

Put the grape concentrate in a bucket together with the juice from the orange and 4 oz sugar. Make up to a gallon with warm water, stirring well.
Proceed as in Beaujolais 1 (page 59), adding the grape juice with the elderflowers.

☐*Not quite so dry, though still very light.*

Liebfraumilch 1

1 can Liebfraumilch Concentrate
1 lb cooking apples
$\frac{1}{2}$ lb fresh grapes
12 oz sugar
1 lb honey
$\frac{1}{4}$ pint white rose petals
yeast nutrient
wine yeast
2 Campden tablets

If you have an electric juicer, extract the juice from the apples in the usual way. If not, chop the apples in a saucepan and pour on a quart of boiling water. Mash with a fork as they soften, and leave for forty-eight hours.
Put the grape concentrate and squeezed grape juice in a bucket, add sugar, and strain on the liquid from the saucepan.
Make up to a gallon with warm water, stirring well.
Proceed as in Beaujolais 1 (page 59).

☐ *This comes somewhere between hock and moselle – not as fruity as the first, not as dry as the second. Many drinkers find it an excellent compromise.*

Liebfraumilch 2

1 can Liebfraumilch Concentrate
1 pint apple juice
4 oz sugar
1 lb honey
¼ pint white rose petals
yeast nutrient
wine yeast
2 Campden tablets

Put the concentrate and sugar in a bucket and make up to a gallon with warm water, stirring well.
Proceed as in Beaujolais 1 (page 59), adding apple juice with the rose petals.

☐*A rather dryer version using apple juice (which is more convenient but more expensive).*

Graves 1

1 can Graves Concentrate
2 bananas
1 lb fresh greengages
1 lb honey
4 oz sugar
¼ pint white rose petals
yeast nutrient
wine yeast
2 Campden tablets
pectozyme

Put the stoned plums in a saucepan with sliced bananas, cover with boiling water and leave for forty-eight hours. Add pectozyme when cool.
Put the concentrate in a bucket with sugar, strain on the liquid from the bananas and greengages and make up to a gallon with warm water. Proceed as in Beaujolais 1 (page 59).

☐ *A smooth, easy wine. It is not fruity like hock, but has plenty of body, and goes well with spicy dishes, like curried chicken where a rather bland partner is called for.*

Graves 2

1 can Graves Concentrate
2 bananas
½ lb canned peaches
1 lemon
1 lb sugar
yeast nutrient
wine yeast
2 Campden tablets
pectozyme

Mash the peaches in a saucepan with 2 tablespoonfuls of juice, add sliced bananas, cover with boiling water and leave for forty-eight hours. Add pectozyme when cool.
Put the concentrate and lemon juice in a bucket, strain on the liquid from bananas and peaches and proceed as in Beaujolais 1 (page 59).

☐ *When greengages are not available, canned peaches will produce a rather smoother, heavier wine – very good with dessert.*

Chablis 1

1 can Chablis Concentrate
1 lb fresh green gooseberries
1 lemon
4 oz sugar
1 lb honey
yeast nutrient
wine yeast
2 Campden tablets
Pectozyme

Top and tail the gooseberries, cover with boiling water and leave for forty-eight hours. Mash the gooseberries as they soften. Add pectozyme when cool.

Put the concentrate, lemon juice and sugar in a bucket, add a quart of hot water and stir well.

Strain on the liquid from the gooseberries and proceed as in Beaujolais 1 (page 59).

☐*Another white wine that almost tingles with dryness. The flavour is light and delicate and goes beautifully with the richer fish dishes.*

Chablis 2

1 can Chablis Concentrate
2 pints grape juice (white)
1 lemon
4 oz sugar
1 lb honey
yeast nutrient
wine yeast
2 Campden tablets

Put the concentrate in a bucket with the juice from the lemon and the sugar, add a quart of hot water and stir well. Make up to a gallon and proceed as in Beaujolais 1 (page 59).
The grape juice should be added two or three days after the honey.

☐ *When fresh gooseberries are not available, a rather extravagant quantity of Schloer grape juice makes this excellent alternative.*

Sauternes 1

1 can Sauternes Concentrate
2 lbs parsnips
1 lb bananas
1½ lbs sugar
¾ pint rose petals or elderberries
(or approximately ¼ oz dried elderflowers)
yeast nutrient
wine yeast
2 Campden tablets
pectozyme

Wash and chop up parsnips. Put in a saucepan, together with the sliced bananas, cover with boiling water and simmer for half an hour.
Leave for forty-eight hours, adding the pectozyme when cool.
Put the grape concentrate and ½ lb of sugar in bucket, add a quart of hot water and stir well. Strain on the liquid from the parsnips and bananas, make up to a gallon and proceed as in Beaujolais 1 (page 59). The remaining pound of sugar should be added in two doses, leaving three days between each.

☐*This is a sweet, even a very sweet dessert wine; and like most sweet wines is surer of success than the lighter, drier varieties. It is almost silky in its smoothness and requires rather more than the usual extra ingredients: a sauternes without a lot of body and a lot of bouquet can be no relation to the French original. In this case, if no fresh elderflowers or rose petals are available, I would recommend dried elderflowers – they are not ideal, but better than nothing.*

Sauternes 2

1 can Sauternes Concentrate
1 lb canned apricots
1 lb bananas
¾ pint elderflowers or rose petals
(or approximately ¼ oz dried elderflowers)
1½ lbs sugar
yeast nutrient
wine yeast
2 Campden tablets
pectozyme

Mash the apricots in one or two tablespoonfuls of juice from the can
and put in a saucepan with mashed bananas. Cover with boiling water
and leave for forty-eight hours. Add pectozyme as soon as the liquid
has cooled.
Proceed as in Sauternes 1 (page 79).

☐ *Although parsnips are around for quite a lot of the year canned
apricots will also do well, giving a rather fruitier flavour.*

Champagne 1

1 can Champagne Concentrate
2 lbs fresh green gooseberries
½ pint Schloer apple juice
1 lb honey
yeast nutrient
champagne yeast
2 Campden tablets
pectozyme

Top and tail the gooseberries, put in a saucepan and cover with boiling water. Mash them as they soften. Leave for forty-eight hours, adding pectozyme as soon as the liquid is cool.

Put the concentrate in a bucket, strain on the liquid from the gooseberries and proceed as in Beaujolais 1 (page 59). Add apple juice 2 days after honey.

There are now three ways to add the sparkle, and these are described on page 83.

☐ *This is unlikely to be confused with a really good French vintage; nevertheless it compares well with some of the less reputable stuff handed out at many weddings and parties. It's light and agreeable on its own and is excellent for champagne cocktails or champagne cup. Basically you are making a dry white wine and adding a sparkle when the fermentation is over: this is not the way they do it in France, but it is a far simpler and safer method for the amateur.*

Champagne 2

1 can Champagne Concentrate
2 oz canned pears
½ pint Schloer apple juice
1 lb honey
yeast nutrient
champagne yeast
2 Campden tablets
pectozyme

Mash the pears in a saucepan with two tablespoonfuls of juice from the can, cover with boiling water and leave for forty-eight hours. Add pectozyme as soon as the liquid is cool.
Put the concentrate in a bucket and proceed as in Champagne 1 (page 81).

☐*If fresh green gooseberries are elusive, the best alternative is canned pears. The flavour is not quite as light, but very pleasant.*

Adding Sparkle

Method 1
This has already been described in the recipe for sparkling rosé (see page 68), and is identical for champagne.

Method 2
If you have a Sparklets siphon, a more instant sparkle is possible. Chill wine; then, with the plastic sleeve in position in the neck of the siphon, pour in the wine until it is close to the top. Insert the siphon tube, screw on the head, charge the siphon with a Sparklets bulb and shake hard. The siphon may be returned to the refrigerator if further chilling is necessary.

When it comes to discharging the liquid, turn the siphon upside down over a sink, see that the end of the siphon tube projects *above* the liquid, and get rid of excess gas by pressing the lever. Turn the siphon upright, unscrew the head, remove the plastic sleeve and pour.

Method 3
Simplest (but unluckily most expensive method) depends on a Soda-stream. This gadget is also very useful for making soda water, tonic, bitter lemon, ginger beer, coca-cola and others; so if you and your family are in the market for these, you could call it a long term economy. But the initial investment (well over £10) is high.

If you do have a Sodastream, all you do is put the wine in the bottles provided and chill them *very thoroughly*. This is important because room temperature wine will overflow, madly, once you start pumping in the gas. Half an hour to an hour in a deep freeze is ideal.

Once this has been done, you simply follow the Sodastream instructions – sliding the bottle into the holder, locking it shut, pumping in the gas with the lever until an escaping hiss says 'enough'. It is then safer to leave the bottle for five minutes before pressing the relief button which gets rid of the gas. Your champagne is ready.

Retsina

1 can Vermouth Type concentrate (red or white)
1 can ordinary grape concentrate (red or white)
2¼ lbs sugar
yeast nutrient
wine yeast
4 Campden tablets

The two cans of concentrate have to be made up separately. Follow the basic winemaking procedure for both using two buckets. Make each up to a gallon with warm water and add activated yeast.

Ferment for three days, then add 12 oz sugar, plus nutrient, to the bucket containing the ordinary grape concentrate and the same amount to the bucket containing the Vermouth concentrate. Ferment for another four days. The ordinary grape concentrate can now be siphoned off in the usual way into a gallon jar with 2 Campden tablets added and an airlock fitted. The Vermouth, however, requires two more doses of sugar: add 6 oz immediately, and 6 oz four days later. Leave for a week, then siphon into a jar, add 2 Campden tablets and fit an airlock.

Both wines should be left for about three months, then racked again. You should now blend the two wines together; but remember, the vermouth is very strong tasting and only a small amount is needed to flavour the ordinary wine. For my own taste, I never use more than a tablespoonful of vermouth to a pint of ordinary wine, red or white. This is quite enough to produce a 'cheat retsina' flavour.

Incidentally, if you do like this taste, you will find the vermouth a great ally with any wines that develop 'off' flavours. It is so strong that even a tiny amount will take over an entire gallon of a not-so-satisfactory vintage.

☐ *This Greek wine, flavoured with resin, is something of an acquired taste but the number of its devotees appears to be growing. In Greece it is made by adding natural pine resin to the fermenting grape juice; but although the principle is quite simple, resin is not an easy substance to handle – and moreover is not easy to lay hands on in England.*

7. How to Fool the Wine Snobs

How to Fool the Wine Snobs

The basic blending routine, described in Chapter 5, should ensure that the raw edge is taken off your young wines. This is the first and most important step; and if you are only interested in producing Vin Ordinaire, it's all that needs to be done. If, however, you want to go grander: if, say, you are throwing a lavish dinner party with guests who are – or claim to be – knowledgeable about wine, then you might like to try a follow-up technique. It's a blatant cheat, but it's surprising how well it can fool people.

This technique differs from basic blending in two respects:

1) Instead of blending opposites – i.e. the very sweet with the very dry, etc. – you blend like with like.

2) The action should be taken *as soon as possible before the wine is drunk,* and certain temperature rules should be observed.

The principle is dead simple. You top up homemade wine with the equivalent commercial wine: three parts of homemade to one part of commercial. It's best to do it in the glass, but it can also be done very satisfactorily in the decanter. If this topping up happens too far ahead of the dinner, the flavour of the old wine tends to get lost in the new. But if the temperature of both wines is right, the short term effects of the blend are almost miraculous – with the taste and bouquet of the older wine permeating the whole of the glass or the decanter. The technique works with any wine type, but best of all with the stronger flavoured ones, like Châteauneuf du Pape, or hock.

Suppose your dinner party begins with a fish dish, and you would like a hock to go with it: shortly before you all sit down to eat, take large wineglasses and fill them three-quarters full of your own hock *well chilled*. Then top up with a commercial hock that is *room temperature*. Chilling a wine does, to some extent, subdue the flavour, so the commercial flavour will be as dominant as possible.

You cannot, of course, continue with the wineglass technique throughout the meal. You must progress to the decanter, using the same proportions – i.e. three-quarters homemade to one quarter commercial; and you must also remember that the temperature rules for the red wines are the same – though higher – as those for the white wines. Your own red has to be slightly under room temperature, whereas the commercial brand must be *well warmed* to bring out its maximum flavour.

Remember, too, that taste buds get duller after a certain amount of food and alcohol. (A French wine taster told me that he could never conceivably do his job at the end of a meal.) So if the first glass is good, really good, then the battle is more than half won; and I think this is a good reason for making the first glass a big one.

One must also be careful every time a different wine with a different flavour is introduced. The burgundy, following on the hock, will need to be well blended: and the same applies to a dessert wine following on the burgundy. It's the second and third glasses of the *same* wine that will begin to pass unnoticed; and here, if the commercial brand begins to run low, you can begin increasing the proportions of your own.

My husband has dubbed it the 'stretch-a-bottle-technique', which is a pretty good description. It does allow you to stretch one good bottle of commercial wine into four, or a half bottle into two, and this is quite a saving.

As well as the lavish dinner parties, you will probably have occasions which are somewhat betwixt and between. There are friends and relations who come so regularly (one might say so relentlessly) that one cannot be expected to make every meal a gala. Still, it isn't *quite* the run-of-the-mill weekday supper, and you have to allow for this both in food and wine. You may not want to 'stretch' a really good bottle or half-bottle of commercial wine; so the compromise is to blend your own Vin Ordinaire with a strongly flavoured commercial brand which is not too expensive. The Bulgarian red wine, Cabernet, or white wine, Chardonnay, do very well; so do many of the Algerian and Chilean vintages. They are relatively cheap, but they are good at imparting a strongly wine-like flavour.

You may find, too, that you have a good bottle of commercial wine to 'stretch' and no homemade equivalent to stretch it into. At a pinch, you can use your Vin Ordinaire; but try to keep on hand a light red (like beaujolais, or even rosé) and a light white (like chablis or moselle). These are excellent blenders because their own flavour is unobtrusive and they take on, very readily, the character of the grand brand.

If you are in any doubt about the colour of your wine, lay on some coloured glassware. You are unlikely to have any problems with the red; but the rosé can sometimes be a little on the mauve side, and most concentrates, with the exception of Southern Vinyards, produce white wines that are not nearly as white as they should be. This doesn't affect the taste, but guests may still recoil from a chablis the colour of a medium-sweet sherry. Pour it into tinted glasses, and who's to know? (If we're going to cheat, let's do the thing in style!)

A surprising number of good and experienced winemakers have told me that they 'wouldn't dare to bring out their own wines at dinner parties' and maybe this is because there are so many wine snobs around. We offer our own moules marinière with pride – who would want to admit that it had been sent round by the local fish-and-chip shop? – yet we cannot rid ourselves of the suspicion that offering homemade wines, like hunting south of the Thames, is socially unacceptable.

Don't believe it
First of all, you needn't tell them and they won't guess if you keep your wine-making equipment out of sight. Secondly, wines are only unacceptable when they taste unexpected and unfamiliar. If *your* wines taste pretty well the way your friends expect a wine to taste, the sensible ones will be overcome by your brilliance at producing it – particularly when they hear what it cost. The wine snobs will carp, but they're not always as clever as they think they are.

True Life Story
A real snob, the kind who insists on smelling the cork when he orders
wine at a restaurant, was invited to try some champagne. A friend
told him it was being offered at a very good price, and his opinion
would be appreciated. After rolling it around, and comparing it to
every champagne vintage under the sun, he concluded it would be
a very good buy for £3 a bottle.

He was drinking a mixture of sherry and tonic water.

*The artist H. M. Bateman was expert at puncturing pretensions of every
kind. This, and the two preceding drawings, show his opinion of wine
snobs.*

8. The Legal Position

The Legal Position

We are now coming to the section of the book which deals with stronger wines and spirits; and as the law comes into this, it might be as well to begin with a summary of what is and is not legal. The following applies to the United Kingdom, so if you live elsewhere you should check on the local situation.

It is legal
to make wines or beers of any strength provided – and this is the crux – provided the alcoholic content is created by the interaction of yeast and sugar. This is a limiting factor because yeast can only tolerate a certain level of alcohol and it is very unlikely to produce wines with an alcoholic content in excess of 20% (or in other words, of about half the strength of conventional whisky or gin).

You can increase the alcoholic content by the addition of bought spirits, on which duty has been paid.
You can drink your own products when and where you like, and you can give them as presents to your friends.

It is NOT legal
to sell anything alcoholic without a licence, and the implications of this go further than you may realise. You cannot even *give* wine away if there are any financial strings attached.
For example, if you run a hotel or restaurant, you cannot give your own wines, free, with the meal because this would be considered a financial advantage for your business in general. You cannot even give your own wines to be raffled, say, in aid of a charity because although *you* are not getting a financial advantage, someone else is. For the same reason, it is illegal to provide your own wines or beers at a dance or social occasion designed to raise money for any cause, however good. If it's purely social, designed for nothing but pleasure, you're in the clear.

Home distilling, as most people know, is strictly illegal in the United Kingdom and in most other countries. Distilling is a heat method that separates the water from the alcohol, thereby creating a liquid with a very much higher alcoholic content – i.e. spirits rather than wine. The more water is taken away, the stronger the liquid becomes. This is illegal, not just because the government likes to grab its enormous tax on spirits, but because there are some real dangers in the process. Distillation, unless it is expertly done, can produce spirits with a harmful balance of ingredients: there can, for instance, be an excess of fusel oil and methyl alcohol which is actively poisonous. Amateur distillers are playing with fire, and risking side effects like blindness or worse – not to mention a prison sentence.

There is another method of strengthening wine which works in precisely the opposite way to distillation, by freezing as opposed to heating. If wine is exposed to a very cold temperature, for instance in a deep freeze, the water freezes solid but the alcohol remains liquid. This, then, is another way of separating water from alcohol and I shall discuss it more fully in Chapter 10.

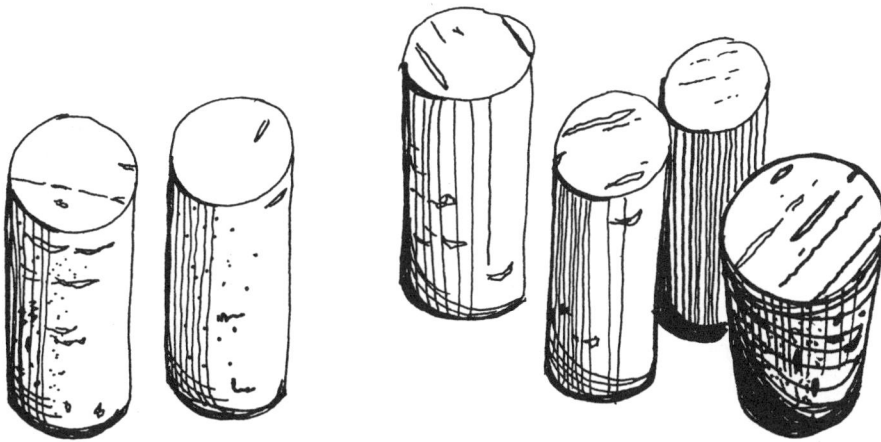

The law does not seem very clear whether this process is permissible in the home or not; and perhaps the reason is because nobody knows just how effectively it works. The facts about distillation are well established; but there are no clear answers to questions like – 'how strong can this freezer technique make a wine? 70° proof, 80° proof, or what?' or 'will it leave impurities in the alcohol?' or 'are there any other bad side effects?' If it *is* illegal, then no one – except, presumably, Customs and Excise – can experiment in order to find out the answers. One can guess that, if you freeze a pint of wine, and extract half a pint of liquid, then this liquid will be twice as strong as the original wine; but it is only a guess.

You will have realised by now that the stronger wines for aperitifs and liqueurs are not quite as straightforward as table wines! But take heart – there *are* ways round as you will see in the next two chapters.

9. Sherry, Port, Vermouth, Madeira and other Stronger Wines

Sherry, Port, Vermouth, Madeira and other Stronger Wines

This group of wines does not present any real problems. There are ways of cosseting a fermentation so that the wine yeast produces an alcoholic content of around 18% or even 20%, and this is reasonably close to the strength of commercial sherry, port and so on.

The alcoholic content of commercial wines and spirits is usually assessed on the bottle in terms of 'proof spirit', and as proof spirit is often confused with alcoholic content, we'd better define the difference. Proof spirit contains 57·1 (or four-sevenths) pure alcohol, so when a bottle of whisky describes itself as 70° proof spirit, it means the alcoholic content is 40%. And the strongest vodka, or 140° proof spirit, means an alcoholic content of 80%.

It is obvious that no wine yeast can produce anything comparable to gin and whisky. But with a little judicious blending, plus small additions of 140° proof Polish spirit, it is possible to produce sherry, vermouth, Dubonnet, madeira and port of genuinely commercial strength.

When I talk about brands like Dubonnet I do not, of course, mean that one can produce the true commercial brand. Their recipes are closely guarded secrets, and one can only talk about flavours that seem to be of the same type.

Fortified wines are among the most rewarding things you can make. The basic cost is no higher than for table wines; and although you will have to be more extravagant with the blending, the saving should be really dramatic. Many people consider the sherry, port and vermouth concentrates to be the most successful in the entire range, and the extra time and trouble is quite manageable.

Extra Equipment
Fortified wines are made in much the same way as ordinary table wines, and you will continue to use the same basic equipment. But we are reaching a stage when two extra items – the filter and the hydrometer – become desirable.

Filters
A filter, as I said in Chapter 3, does not make an enormous difference to red wines. (So if you're only interested in ruby port, there's no need to worry.) But a pale sherry or a white vermouth can benefit a great deal; and the majority of winemakers agree that this is the moment when a filter becomes a worthwhile investment. (You will also need it for a Poor Man's Spirits and for more advanced winemaking.)

The object is to remove all particles, however small, from the liquid. At its simplest, you can pour the wine through a kitchen funnel lined with filter paper: but this is slow and laborious and doesn't seem to get the best results.

There are various brands of filters on the market, all of which do the job efficiently. I find the Southern Vinyards Vinbrite Wine Filter is, perhaps, easier to handle – although I would recommend everyone to carry out the operation in the bath tub. Filtering just does seem to be a slightly drippy, messy business and one ought to be prepared for this.

The Vinbrite Filter siphons the wine from one jar into another; and in the process, the liquid passes through a thick, slightly fluffy pad. It takes time, but this pad certainly seems to trap the haze-forming particles, and the wine emerges shiningly and transparently clear. A comparison of the liquid before and after can be very dramatic.

The Hydrometer and the sugar feeding method
The second piece of equipment is the hydrometer. This, too, was rated non-essential in Chapter 3; but now that it is necessary to convert the maximum amount of sugar into alcohol, the usefulness of this instrument becomes undeniable.

Table wines, as you will remember, can take their supplementary sugar in one or two large doses; but when you are hoping to push the alcoholic content up above 14% or 15%, it is advisable to add the sugar little by little rather than all at once. This gradual feeding keeps the yeast active for a longer period. The hydrometer helps because it can tell you precisely *when* to add these small doses of sugar, and when to stop.

Let's take a closer look at the instrument. In appearance, the hydrometer is rather like a thermometer with a weighted bottom. It carries a range of figures beginning with around 0·990 at the top, and going to 1·150 at the bottom. (Being a scientific instrument, it works the opposite way to what you would expect: the figures go down as the instrument goes up!)

When you want to measure the sugar content of a liquid, you put a sample in a tall, thin container and lower the hydrometer inside, spinning it a little to get rid of the bubbles.

Hydrometer readings should always be taken with the eye level with the surface of the liquid. Never look down on it.

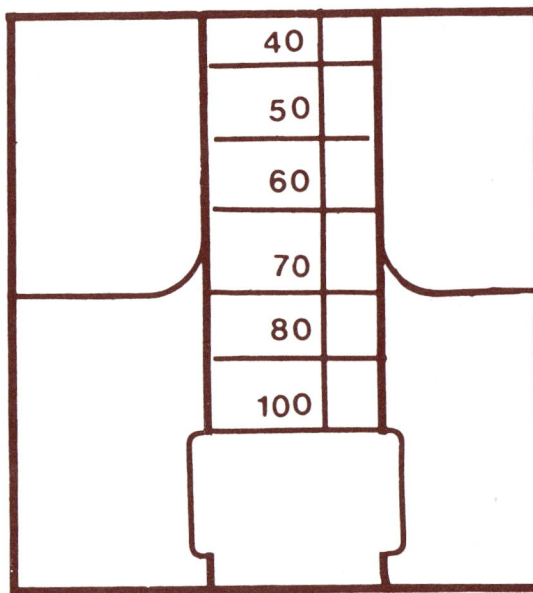

If the liquid is sweet – containing, about 3 lbs sugar per gallon – the hydrometer will float high with the figure 1·110 coinciding with the top of the liquid. If there is no sugar at all, as in plain water, the hydrometer will plummet.

The hydrometer doesn't do anything as simple as tell you, in pounds and ounces, how much sugar is present; but, as an approximate guide, you can reckon that anything under 1·000 means no sugar, that 1·035 means 1 lb sugar, that 1·075 means 2 lbs, 1·110, 3 lbs, and 1·150, 4 lbs. To put it another way, every three points represents slightly more than an ounce.

It is important to know how much sugar has gone into your wine, but you don't need a hydrometer to assess this. (See pages 33–4.) What is useful is that the hydrometer will tell you exactly what is happening to the sugar during fermentation. Your own taste is a good general guide; but in the later stages, when one is coaxing the yeast to stay alive with gradual sugar feeding, it is not precise enough. When the rate of conversion to alcohol is very slow, you may not be able to taste that anything is happening at all; but the hydrometer can always tell. Every time it registers a drop, however small, in points, you know the yeast is still active: when it stays fast at the same point, you know the yeast has given up and there's no point adding any more sugar.

The hydrometer tells you when to stop; and it also helps you to assess when is the best moment to add another dose of sugar to a still active fermentation. The simplest technique is to establish a point on the hydrometer which says, in effect, 'next dose, please'.

The technique can be the same for all stronger wines – sweet, medium-sweet or dry. (As with table wines, the best principle is to start dry and sweeten to taste later.) And although there are no fixed rules, I have found the following system to work pretty well. Start with 2 lbs sugar in a gallon of liquid: then add 4 oz sugar every time the hydrometer reading touches 1·010. Do this about four times. Thereafter, cut the dose to 2 oz and add it when the point is just over 1·000. Go on doing this until the hydrometer sticks fast on one point for a week or so. Then stop.

In the early stages, the hydrometer will register a fast drop as the yeast will be at its most active. This will slow down considerably after you've fed in the first pound of sugar – could indeed stick at any moment. You'll be doing well if you persuade the yeast to accept a further 8 oz or 12 oz, and this will mean an alcoholic content of around 18%.

If you feel this is all too much trouble, and that you'd rather risk a lower-than-best alcoholic content, you can still make out quite well with your taste-testing. Begin, in the same way, with a total of 2 lbs sugar per gallon, and keep adding 4 oz every three or four days. Begin to go cautiously after you've added 1 lb, cutting the dose to 2 oz and never adding this unless the wine tastes reasonably dry. When the wine seems to stay rather sweet for a week on end, stop. You may find you have over-sweetened a dry sherry, but blending with a super-dry commercial sherry should put this right.

Invert Sugar

The reasons for using invert sugar have already been given (see page 57) and although the difference it makes may not be enormous, one should use all the help one can get.

Honey, the natural 'invert', is excellent though not quite so easy to measure out in small doses as ordinary sugar. I usually add a quarter of a 1 lb pot at a time, which is the equivalent of 3 oz sugar.

You can invert sugar yourself by taking 2 lbs granulated sugar, adding ½ pint of water and ¼ teaspoonful of citric acid, bringing to the boil and simmering for twenty minutes. When the liquid turns a pale straw colour, add another ½ pint of cold water. You will now find you have about 2 pints of syrup, each pint being equivalent to 1 lb sugar. The correct amount of sugar can be measured out, near enough, in tablespoonfuls: 2 oz sugar equalling about 5 tablespoonfuls of syrup.
Always mix both honey and invert sugar in a little warm water before adding to the wine.

Added spirit
Polish spirit or vodka is usually recommended because the colour and taste are neutral and – being 140° proof – only very small quantities are needed. You can reckon, for example, that one tablespoonful of Polish vodka will increase the alcoholic content of a bottle of wine by about 1½%. This spirit costs over £6 a bottle, so obviously it should be used with extreme discretion, and there are many winemakers who feel that it is unnecessary to use it at all. If the sherry or port *tastes* right, very few people are going to notice if the strength is a little under the commercial equivalent. The decision to add, or not to add, is very much up to the individual; and my own feeling is that it pays to be extravagant with the blending rather than the spirit. Sandeman will do far more for your own port than tablespoonfuls of vodka.
There is, however, one point about sherry that has to be kept in mind. Unlike other white wines, sherry needs air, for unless it is 'oxidised', it will refuse to develop anything like the authentic flavour. In practice, this means that you must always plug the maturing wine with cotton wool and never fill the jar more than seven-eighths full; and this, of course, means that there is a danger of infection from bacteria. The stronger the wine, the less the danger – whoever heard of gin going bad? – so there is an argument for saying that sherry needs some added spirit as a protection. I have, for this reason, included Polish spirit in the sherry recipes; but I must also say that I and many other winemakers have made sherry very successfully without this precaution, so if your fermentation has gone well, you can look on it as an optional extra.

It has already been made clear that the blending operation is even more crucial with fortified than with table wines. Never forget that fortified wines will probably be drunk on their own, without any good food to help disguise imperfections; and although the blending principles are exactly the same, you may find that it pays to add more than the standard one part commercial to three parts homemade. I have found that this is particularly true of dry sherry.

Once again, though, this is a matter for your own taste, and the taste of your friends, to decide.

Italian Vermouth (sweet)

This is a case where extra ingredients are frankly unnecessary. The sweet Vermouth Concentrate (red or white) has been extremely successful at capturing the bitter herb flavour associated with vermouth; and added herbs only exaggerate the taste to an undesirable extent.

The CWE brand is excellent. Simply put concentrate in a bucket, make up to a gallon, add yeast and proceed in the usual way, adding $2\frac{1}{2}$ lbs sugar in gradual doses. After fermentation, the final sweetening can be done with sugar; but as always, I prefer to do at least part of it with commercial Italian vermouth.

French Vermouth (dry)

Once again I find the concentrate very satisfactory. The juice of two lemons, added during fermentation, is all to the good; but apart from this, no extras are needed.

The method is the same as for Italian Vermouth, also adding $2\frac{1}{2}$ lbs sugar.

Dry Sherry

1 can Pale Sherry Concentrate
2 bananas
2 dessertspoonfuls tea leaves (1 China, 1 Indian)
2 lbs honey
sherry yeast
yeast nutrient
1 tablespoonful 140° Polish spirit (optional)

Gently boil the bananas in their skins for twenty minutes. Make tea in a large pot with boiling water (about a pint) in which four table-spoonfuls of honey have been dissolved. Allow to cool.

Put the concentrate and $\frac{1}{2}$ lb of honey in a bucket, strain on the boiling water from the bananas and stir well. Add cold tea, also strained, and make up to a gallon.

Add the yeast, cover the bucket, and if possible leave at a temperature in the low sixties.

Follow the slow sugar-feeding method, with the help of a hydrometer, as described earlier in the chapter (page 97). Half a teaspoonful of nutrient should be added twice towards the end of the fermentation.

When all the sugar has been added and the specific gravity is close to 1·000, siphon the sherry into a gallon jar. By this time the liquid should have reduced to about $\frac{7}{8}$ of a gallon so the jar will not be full, but no topping up is necessary as sherry needs oxidation.

Plug the jar with cotton wool and leave in a cool place for three months. During this period the sherry flor should appear. This begins as islands of yeast on the surface of the liquid, and a full blown sherry flor – such as they would get in Spain – will develop into something that looks like a covering of cheese with yeast hanging down underneath in stringy lumps. You may not get anything so dramatic, but there should be some surface cover; and the sherry should not be touched until all has subsided.

When all is calm and clear, add a tablespoonful of Polish spirit, leave for a further week or two, and siphon into bottles.

Blend in the glass with a few drops of brandy and a dry commercial sherry – one part commercial to three parts of your own.

☐ *As usual, the dry variety is the hardest to emulate. The sherry concentrates make pleasant tasting wines, reminiscent of sherry – but not reminiscent enough. Extra ingredients improve the quality and flavour, but blending with commercial sherry is necessary if this is to be presented as the real thing to your friends.*

Medium Sherry

The recipe is the same as for Dry Sherry, but use a Medium Sherry Concentrate, and two tablespoonfuls instead of two dessertspoonfuls of tea leaves – China and Indian. Half a pint of Schloer Apple Juice, added at the end of the fermentation, will help the flavour.

Blend with commercial sherry in the same way – but use a rather sweet variety to bring the sherry from dry to medium.

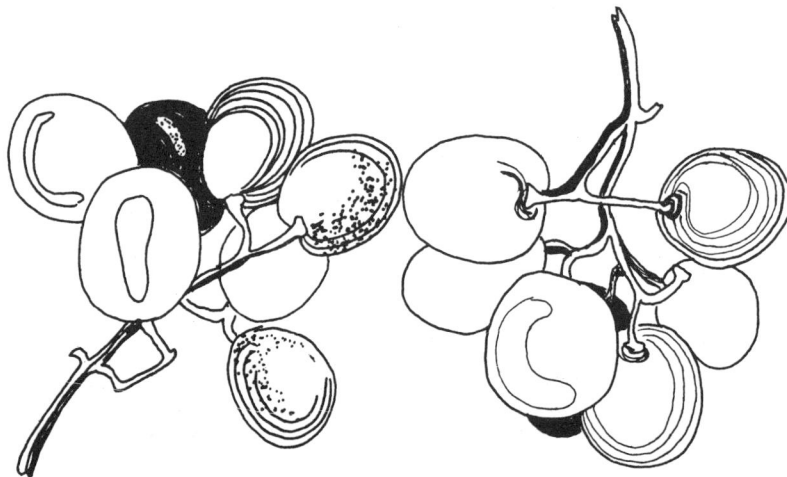

Cream Sherry

1 can Cream Sherry Concentrate
3 bananas
1 lb dried apricots
2½ lbs brown sugar
sherry yeast
yeast nutrient
1 tablespoonful Polish spirit (optional)
pectozyme

Put the apricots and sliced bananas in a saucepan, sprinkle on 1 lb brown sugar, cover with boiling water and leave for forty-eight hours. Add a tablespoonful of pectozyme as soon as the liquid is cool.

Put the concentrate in a bucket, strain on the liquid from the apricots and proceed as with Dry Sherry (page 104).

Specific gravity will, of course, be higher at the end of fermentation – perhaps around 1·010.

If it is too syrupy, blend with a drier commercial sherry; otherwise, use another cream variety.

☐*If you have a sweet tooth, this sherry is very successful and requires rather less blending than the other two.*

Port 1 (full and sweet)

1 can Port Concentrate
1 can Grape and Elderberry Concentrate
3 bananas
1 tablespoonful Ribena or other blackcurrant syrup
2 lbs sugar
port yeast
yeast nutrient
2 Campden tablets

Slice the bananas, cover with boiling water and leave for twenty-four hours.

Put the concentrate and blackcurrant syrup in a bucket, strain on the liquid from the bananas and proceed in the usual way.

Rack four times, at three monthly intervals, and bottle for use. Blend as for sherry.

☐ *This can fool a lot of people, particularly if you keep it for a year and blend with a good commercial port.*

Port 2 (rather lighter)

1 can Port Concentrate
1 can Grape and Bilberry Concentrate
Juice from 7 oz can of blackberries
port yeast
yeast nutrient
1½ lbs sugar
2 Campden tablets

Put concentrate and blackberry juice in a bucket, make up to a gallon and proceed as usual.

This port can be drunk rather sooner – after the third racking. Blend with a tawny port.

Madeira

I must hand a bouquet to Southern Vinyards and say that I think it would be very difficult to improve on their Madeira Concentrate. It will not, of course, come out as strong as the commercial equivalent but the flavour is really delightful. You can simply follow the instructions on the container; or, if you are aiming for maximum strength, try the slow sugar feeding method.

'Cheat' Dubonnet

A slight quinine flavour characterises the French Dubonnet, obtained from Cinchona bark. Cinchona essence is available at most wine-making stores and, like the vermouth herbs in the concentrate, is very effective. 'Cheat' Dubonnet is made like a liqueur and, as you will see, the method is rather different.

Measure 1 fluid oz (or 2 tablespoonfuls) 140° proof Polish spirit into a jug, add 4 or 5 drops of Cinchona essence and mix well. Add 3 oz (or 6 tablespoonfuls) sugar syrup. This syrup is prepared like invert sugar, except that you add a full pint of water to 2 lbs sugar, boil for only a few moments until solution is clear, and then allow to cool. No citric acid is needed.

Now put the Polish spirit, mixed with Cinchona essence and sugar syrup, into a bottle and top up with one of your own red wines. A strong, fruity one – like Burgundy 1 (page 61) – is good; possibly treated with the freezer method (pages 93–4).

'Cheat' Campari

It is not practical to give a recipe, even for a cheat version of Campari because the necessary herbs are not available in England. At the moment, there is no concentrate available either; but I have sampled experiments both at CWE and Southern Vinyards and am convinced that, if either chose to go ahead and produce it, the result would be a great and economical joy to the Campari-lover. Neither firm is convinced that there is a big enough market for this rather special aperitif; but if any of my readers feel otherwise, do write to one or other and try to persuade them otherwise.

10. Poor Man's Whisky, Gin, Brandy and Liqueurs

Poor Man's Whisky, Gin, Brandy and Liqueurs

Legends persist about dandelion wine as potent as whisky, and beetroot port with the kick of a five-star brandy; but these are legends, not facts. You will know by now the limitations of a yeast, and how all the cossetting in the world will not persuade it to produce wine more than half as strong as commercial spirits. It is certainly illegal to strengthen your wine by distilling, it is doubtfully legal to strengthen it by the freezer technique – see Chapter 8 – and it is legal but uneconomic to strengthen with too much 140° proof Polish spirit or vodka.

There are certain liqueurs, like crême de menthe or cherry brandy, which are drunk for their flavour rather than their kick, and these flavours can be made very good without the uneconomic addition of strong spirits. But one cannot get away from it: the great cry is for a poor man's gin or whisky, and most people do not like the idea of it being half strength. It's as well to face the facts squarely if one is to find some realistic ways round, and I'll begin by admitting that there are no less than three problems connected with a poor man's spirits: colour, taste, and strength.

Colour
This problem does not apply to whisky or brandy or rum, but it applies very much to gin and vodka. No one has yet succeeded in making an *absolutely* colourless wine, though some recent experiments have shown me that one can come pretty close. You will always see a difference between the lightest, most exquisitely filtered white wine and a glass of gin if you put them side by side.
There are a number of ways round the problem. Coloured partners with the gin – like tomato juice, ginger ale or bitter lemon – are one solution. Or you can borrow from the techniques in Chapter 7 and put the martini or gin-and-tonic in a tinted glass. This is playing very safe because, realistically, no one is likely to notice the faint colour difference unless they are actively looking for it.

Taste

This is a harder one because there is no such thing as a wine that tastes convincingly like spirits. Various flavourings are available which are said to add the taste of rum, brandy and so on, but although they can help, they are not the complete answer.

The first thing to do is make a wine that is as neutral flavoured as possible, and also very dry. Again, no one has succeeded in making an entirely tasteless wine any more than they have succeeded in making an entirely colourless one; but a very simple recipe has been devised which works pretty well. Having achieved a base wine that is as neutral-coloured and neutral-flavoured as possible, you can experiment with the flavourings mentioned earlier, and these can be bought at most winemaking stores. To get a more authentic taste, one has to go back to the old blending principle – three parts homemade wine to one part commercial spirits. As with table wines, last minute blending works best, and you should get the wine *as cold as possible* to subdue any flavour as much as possible. The heavier, strong-tasting whiskies, brandies, gins, rums make the best blenders, but tasteless vodka is a problem for which there is no real solution.

Strength

If the wine ferments well, and if you add 4 oz or 8 tablespoonfuls of Polish spirit per bottle, you should end up with something that is around 25% weaker than conventional gin or whisky at a cost of slightly over £1. A further 2 oz spirit would cost about 50p more, but the wine might then be as little as 10% weaker. Still another ounce or two might even bring you above the commercial strength; but at £2 a bottle, this hardly qualifies as a poor man's spirits.

It is also possible, as we already know, to increase the alcohol content of wine by what is known as the 'freezer method'. Briefly, this involves subjecting the wine to a sub-zero temperature for several hours, for instance in the coldest part of a deep freeze. This causes part of the water in the wine to separate off as ice, which can be removed, leaving a much stronger residue. Some people claim to have had excellent results this way, but the method is difficult to time and may, like heat distilling, be dangerous. More importantly, **it may be illegal.** Before the days of deep freezes, the technique was hardly practicable, so –

unlike heat distilling which has long been known and strictly controlled – the freezer method of increasing alcoholic strength is a fairly recent development. For this reason a definite legal ruling on the subject does not, at the time of writing, appear to exist, though official minds may soon be made up. So please, if you are tempted to experiment, first check the legal situation whether in the UK or elsewhere. (For a general discussion on how the law affects home winemaking, please see pages 92–4.)

However, it is surprising how many people find that a 10% to 25% lower than usual strength doesn't really worry them. As with sherry and port, the right taste is of enormous importance; and if you achieve one you like, a slight lowering of the spirit level may not seem to matter. And after all, a wine of 30% alcohol isn't by any means weak!

Conclusion
A poor man's vodka really isn't practicable, and I wouldn't advise anyone to waste time attempting it. The whisky, gin, rum and brandy are well worth trying.

I must be honest, however, and admit that the 'spirits bluff' does not work as well as the 'wine bluff.' Wine snobs can be fooled with remarkable ease; but anyone with a fondness for whisky is unlikely to confuse your poor man's offering with the real thing if offered a straight comparison. Most people, myself included, find that our home-made varieties work best in long drinks or cocktails or party cups. A whisky sour is safer than a simple scotch on the rocks, a brandy and ginger ale is safer than just brandy, and so on and so forth. When there is an extra flavouring, or flavourings, at work, the poor man's spirits can become genuinely indistinguishable; but when the only addition is a little ice and water, they are less likely to pass muster. As with table wines, it's as well to involve other people in taste-testing so that you can be reasonably confident of their acceptability. You yourself may get accustomed to a whisky flavour or a gin strength that is quite unrelated to the commercial equivalents, but friends can never be relied on to share a new taste. They might appreciate a lemon-coloured martini with an unfamiliar flavour and half the usual strength. On the other hand, they might not.

Poor Man's Gin

First, you must make your 'base wine' and this should be as light-coloured and light-flavoured as possible. It should also be inexpensive. A plain sugar wine would be ideal, but I have not found that it ferments out reliably unless there is some proportion of grape concentrate. The following recipe uses Southern Vinyards Vin Ordinaire (white) which is a pleasantly light wine; and the colour and flavour are lightened still further by using double quantities of water plus extra sugar.

> 1 pint Southern Vinyards Vin Ordinaire (white)
> 5–6 lbs sugar
> wine yeast
> yeast nutrient
> Campden tablets
> 2 gallons water
> Gin essence

Activate the yeast.
Invert 3 lbs sugar, as described on pages 100–1, and put in a plastic bucket.
Add the grape concentrate and make up to two gallons of liquid.
Add the yeast and 2 teaspoonfuls of yeast nutrient.
Cover the bucket and leave in a warm place. (White wine should usually be fermented out at a slightly lower temperature than red; but in this case, a really warm temperature is desirable – if possible, between 75° and 80°.)
Follow the slow sugar-feeding method described on page 97.
When the maximum sugar has been converted into alcohol, siphon the wine into jars, add 1 Campden tablet per gallon, plug with cotton wool or airlocks, and leave for a month.
Filter the wine into clean jars and leave for a further two months.
The 'base wine' is now ready for use and can be bottled – preferably in old gin bottles! Add eight tablespoonfuls of Polish spirit to each bottle, or twelve if you're feeling extravagant. Add gin essence to taste, and blend three parts to one with commercial gin.

Poor Man's Whisky

Old country recipes usually tell us that wheat wine has a real whisky flavour. Maybe long years of maturing will indeed produce one; but in the short term, the taste of wheat wine is unlikely to be confused with any of the commercial brands. However, I have found that it makes a better base for blending with whisky than a wine made from grape concentrate.

> 1 lb wheat
> two large potatoes (scrubbed clean and sliced)
> 2 lbs raisins
> 3–5 lbs demerara sugar
> 2 lbs malt extract
> wine yeast
> yeast nutrient
> Campden tablets
> 2 gallons water

Activate the yeast.

Soak the wheat overnight in a pint of water, in a plastic bucket.

Add the potatoes, raisins, and 3 lbs sugar, and pour on one gallon of boiling water. Cool to blood heat and add the yeast and 2 teaspoonfuls of yeast nutrient.

Cover the bucket and leave in a warm place, stirring daily.

When the hydrometer reading has dropped to 1·010, dissolve 1 lb malt extract in four pints of warm water and feed the solution to the must, a pint at a time.

After adding the final pint, allow hydrometer reading to drop close to 1·000, then dissolve a further 1 lb malt extract in 4 pints warm water and feed in half a pint at a time.

When all the malt is 'digested', continue sugar-feeding with 2 oz-doses of demerara sugar for as long as possible. Keep stirring every day.

Strain the liquid into gallon jars. Ideally, they should be topped up with whisky; but if you think this is too extravagant, plain water will do. Add 1 Campden tablet per gallon. Mature for at least six months, racking into clean jars every three months.

Flavour to taste with whisky essence, and blend three parts to one with commercial whisky.

Poor Man's Brandy and Rum

The 'base wine' is the same as for Poor Man's Gin (page 115).
Flavour with brandy or rum essences, and blend three parts to one
with the commercial spirits.

Liqueurs

It may surprise you to discover that making liqueurs is far and away
the quickest and easiest form of winemaking. It is usually a question
of adding certain ingredients to a basic red or white wine, and this can
sometimes be done in a matter of minutes if fruit extracts are used.
Unlike the flavourings for whisky or gin (which I'm doubtful about)
many of these extracts are very successful.

The strength will mainly come from the added Polish spirit or brandy,
and frankly this is very much a question of what you can or can't
afford. Recipes will give maximum quantities; but as was said earlier,
the flavour will not suffer if you use less, even considerably less.

One of the ingredients will be 'sugar syrup.' This is made by mixing 2
lb granulated sugar with a pint of water, bringing it to the boil, and
leaving it there for a few moments until the liquid becomes clear and
colourless. Cool before use.

Measurements will be given in fluid ounces; and in case you don't have
a jug that gives this scale, just remember that 1 fluid ounce equals two
tablespoonfuls. All the recipes are for one bottle.

Peach Brandy

Measure 9 fluid oz 140° Polish spirit into a jug, add 2 teaspoonfuls Peach Brandy Extract, mix well and pour into an empty bottle. Mix 2 fluid oz of juice from can of peaches with 5 fluid oz sugar syrup and add to bottle. Top up bottle with white wine and shake well. The addition of a little brandy in the glass, immediately before serving, is a great help.

Cherry Brandy

5 fluid oz 140° Polish spirit
4 fluid oz sugar syrup
1 fluid oz juice from can of red cherries
1 teaspoonful Cherry Brandy essence
red wine

The method is the same as for Peach Brandy. (About 44° proof spirit.)

Pineapple Brandy

3 fluid oz 140° Polish spirit
2 fluid oz sugar syrup
2 fluid oz juice from canned pineapple
3 teaspoonfuls Ananas extract (T. Noirot)
White wine

The method is the same as for Peach Brandy. (About 36° proof.)

☐ *If you'd like to try something a little more unusual, this 'brandy' works well. The pineapple flavour is easy to get across, and blends happily with most white wines.*

Sloe Gin

This is more time consuming.

Fill a bottling jar with fresh sloes, pricking each one several times with a fork. Add 10 oz sugar to every pound of sloes. Fill the jar with equal parts of gin and white wine – all gin if you can afford it. Seal the jar and leave for about three months, shaking occasionally and turning upside down. Drain off the liquid and bottle.

Creme de Menthe

4 fluid oz 140° Polish spirit
7 fluid oz sugar syrup
1 to 2 teaspoonfuls Creme de Menthe flavour (Grey Owl)
White wine

The method is the same as for Peach Brandy. (About 37° proof.)

Benedictine

12 fluid oz 140° Polish spirit
4 fluid oz sugar syrup
1 to 2 teaspoonfuls Dictine essence (Grey Owl)
Sauternes type wine

The method is the same as for Peach Brandy. (About 72° proof.)

☐ *This is strong and extravagant.*

11. Advanced Winemaking

Advanced Winemaking

By now, I hope you will have proved by your own experiments that six-week wines, made by the gallon, can taste not just drinkable but good. Still, there is a big difference between 'good' and 'very good' and you may want to progress to the wines which are in the second category. You may also have an idea that advanced winemaking is beyond the amateur, and it must be admitted that certain aspects can sound daunting – especially to those of us who have no head for maths and chemistry. But the most vital principles can be reduced to a reasonable simplicity, and it is on these that I have concentrated.

More than anything, it is a question of time and trouble; but even if you conclude that the extra effort is not for you, I don't think you will have any difficulty in understanding this chapter, or in seeing that advanced winemaking is not just for a handful of experts. Like more sophisticated cooking, it is in reach of anyone who genuinely wants to achieve it.

The methods rather than the ingredients are different, and this is why only five recipes will be discussed: red and white table wines, sherry, port and champagne. In the case of claret, it is true, the proportion of ingredients given in this chapter is different to those in Chapter 5 – because the longer maturing period means that the starting level of tannin can be much higher. But in general, any of the recipes given earlier can be taken and done in the grand manner, and they will all benefit enormously.

Extra Equipment

There is almost no end to what you could buy on this front; but, as before, I have tried to keep the list as minimal as possible. Your own experiments will probably lead you into other buying sprees, and in the long term this can be all to the good. Assuming, however, that this is your first venture into Château-style wines, it still makes sense to follow the same principle as for daily wine and to avoid buying anything that is not *strictly* necessary.

In addition to the items on the Minimum Equipment lists on page 27, you will need:

> Oak cask (the smallest size holds 4½ gallons)
> Large white plastic dustbin with lid (or you might like to buy a special plastic container from a winemaking store. One is now available which marks the level of gallons and ½ gallons, and this is a great help.)
> Hydrometer with measuring jar
> Special wine yeasts
> Citric acid
> Filter

Casks

Why the oak cask? In order to develop the best possible flavour and the best possible bouquet, wine needs slow, gentle oxidation. That is to say, it needs contact with a small but continuously renewed supply of oxygen during a large part of its maturing period. Far and away the best means of securing this is via the walls of an oak cask. Oak is porous, but the pores are so minute that only a small quantity of oxygen, absolutely free of dust and bacteria, can enter. This is exactly what's needed, and no other container can supply it so well.

Frankly it's a pity, because oak casks are expensive to buy, awkward to handle and a perfect devil to clean. But as there is no real substitute, these drawbacks have to be endured. On top of the oxidation benefit, it is also a fact that wine absorbs beneficial substances from the wood and vice versa; so the overall advantages add up formidably.

Care of casks

It is more of a chore – to put it mildly – to clean wood than glass or polythene. Wood retains 'off' flavours and bacteria far more tenaciously, and the happy days when you could swill with disinfectant, swill with water and finish, are gone. When you buy a cask, and most especially if it is second hand, it must be cleaned and sterilised in the following way.

1. Fill with cold water and leave for at least twelve hours to allow the wood to become moist.

2. Pour off water and refill with a hot solution of washing soda – 2 lbs soda to 5 gallons of hot water. Leave for another 12 hours.

3. Empty again, swill out with cold water, re-fill with very hot or, preferably, boiling water and leave for another twelve hours.

4. Empty and rinse until you are sure that the water coming out is both colourless and odourless.

5. Prepare sterilising solution with Campden tablets and citric acid.

   For the $4\frac{1}{2}$ gallon cask, you will need about half a gallon of this solution – i.e. eight Campden tablets and four saltspoonfuls of citric acid dissolved in four pints of water. (Increase proportions for larger casks.) Put solution in cask and swill it round and round for as long as you can bear it.

6. Empty. Rinse for what feels like the eightieth time. And then, ideally, you should 'condition' the cask with a bottle of your own wine to which a teaspoonful of citric acid and a pinch of grape tannin has been added. Roll this around the cask, again for as long as you can bear it, and tip away.

You'll be glad to hear that this appalling process need never be repeated. Every time you empty the cask of your own wine, you need only swill out with cold water – if you re-fill at once with another vintage. The golden rule is *keep the casks full*.

It's also good news that – apart from sherries – white wines do not benefit from oak casks nearly as much as red because oxidation is not, in their case, particularly helpful. It is still better to make them in larger quantities – at least four or five gallons – but they can be matured in glass containers, like carboys, which are much easier to cope with.

The reasons for fermenting wine in larger rather than smaller quantities have already been touched on in other chapters; and it comes down to the simple fact that wine in bulk creates the ideal fermenting temperature. The ideal fermentation, one that contributes best to the ultimate flavour, is slow and steady and long drawn out; and however hard one tries with airing cupboards and submersible water heaters, a small quantity of wine just cannot generate the *consistently* perfect temperature in the same way as five gallons. And ten or twenty do it even better.

A fast fermentation is necessary for a short term wine, but it does undoubtedly dissipate some of the more delicate flavours and bouquets – particularly those of a white wine. Now that our vintages are being allowed to take their time, there is no need to hurry the fermentation period any more than the maturing period. If you can manage it, I would suggest putting the wine in a warm place, like the airing cupboard, at the start of fermentation; but as soon as things get active, move the container to a cooler place – around 65°F.

Racking
This process has to be repeated regularly with most of your best wines.

Claret, for example, must be racked every three months for the whole of its cask life – and this life can run into years. (The exception is sherry which is not racked at all while it is maturing in the cask.)

Each racking gets rid of some residual sediment and helps to clarify the colour. You can, if you like, experiment with wine finings; but I have found they are even less necessary for the best wines than for the daily wines. Racking also brings in an extra dose of oxygen and this, even when the wine is maturing in an oak cask, is good for the developing flavour.

Bottling

There comes a time when wine no longer benefits from oxidation; in fact the development of 'esters' – an element in the wine which contributes most to the final smoothness, delicacy and bouquet – progresses much better in airtight conditions.

Experts admit that it is very difficult to lay down hard and fast rules on the timing of this. But once the wine is *really clear*, once you feel the taste is *really changing*, it's safe to assume that the wine can come out of the cask and into the bottle. Clarets take longer; but most red wines should be ready for bottling after a year or so.

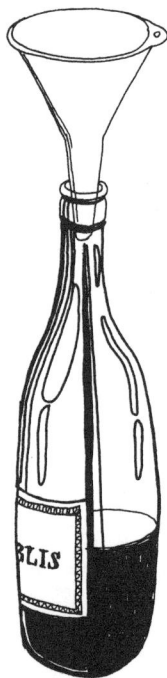

Ageing
Why does a wine develop so many good things as it ages? Even a scientist allows that the reasons are 'exceedingly complex', involving 'innumerable chemical reactions' many of which are 'most imperfectly understood'. In other words, we know it happens: we don't – altogether – know why.

However, a lot *is* known about the conditions and the timing that favour the right development, and these are things that even a layman can understand. One may not be able to grasp why a high percentage of tannin, acid and alcohol, reacting on each other, should create a superb claret flavour, but it's easy enough to see that the process takes time. Some perfectionists would say as long as twenty years. We may not be able to pinpoint the reasons why a hock matures so much quicker but, most evidently, it does.

One can know, in general terms, how long a wine should take to mature; but ultimately, it is one's own judgement that has to decide on the drinking moment. You must taste wine regularly to see how it is coming along, and as soon as your taste tells you it is really good, it's as well to start drinking. It's always interesting to reserve a few bottles for longer periods, to see if they will improve further; but don't forget that wine can easily go over the hill and start deteriorating. Timing, like blending, is not a question of rules and regulations: it's far more a question of your own taste and experience.

The Hydrometer
The hydrometer is useful for your best wines just as it is for stronger wines. The steady, drawn-out fermentation is encouraged by the gradual sugar-feeding method described in Chapter 8; and, as you will have seen, the hydrometer has an important part to play in this. You will also want your best wines to be of exactly the right dryness and the hydrometer, being more exact than your own taste, helps to achieve this.

Filtering
White wines, if left long enough, will sometimes clear themselves perfectly well. But they nearly always benefit from being filtered a month or two after fermentation is complete (see page 97).

Special wine yeasts

Instead of a general purpose wine yeast, you can buy the yeast specially adapted to a particular wine type. These will have been developed from the yeasts on the grapes where, traditionally, the wine type is made; and they are supposed to impart a more authentic flavour to your own vintage.

Opinions differ on their efficiency, and I don't think it can be said that any very dramatic differences are involved. However, I do believe that the improvement, though slight, can be noticeable – especially with port, sherry and champagne; and as the expense is not great, they are certainly worth a try.

Tannin and acidity

In advanced winemaking circles, you are likely to hear how the right degrees of tannin and acidity are essential to a balanced wine. This is perfectly true; but it is also true that the business of assessing and adjusting these elements is frankly beyond most of us – moreover they defy simplification.

At worst, you are called upon to use apparatus like a 1 x 25 ml burette graduated in 0·1 ml divisions. And even Mr Berry's *First Steps in Winemaking*, which does a splendid job in bringing the science of winemaking down to a comprehensible level, is reduced to telling us that . . .

> 'a simple way of testing the acid content of a wine or "must" is to use B.D.H. Narrow Range pH indicator paper (aim at a colour reaction equivalent to between pH3 and 4).'

In these circumstances, I feel that one can only cling to two comforting facts:

1. Grapes have the best balance of tannin and acidity of any fruit. They are not likely to let us down.

2. The grape concentrate experts do test their product very carefully to see if the balance is correct; and if it isn't, they adjust it.

So the short answer is – don't worry. Even if one can't, remotely, cope with scientific tests, one can still hope to make truly excellent wines.

Sherry

Follow any of the three recipes in Chapter 9; but try to include gypsum in the ingredients. (This chemical is not easy to obtain, but chemists will sometimes order it specially for you.) Gypsum is part of the soil in the traditional sherry areas, and it definitely encourages the full-blown sherry flor which produces the best and most authentic flavour. 1 oz gypsum per gallon should be added with the yeast. Mature the wine in a cask for a year – but remember that the cask must not be kept more than three-quarters full. No racking is necessary until the wine is bottled.

Claret

5 cans Claret Concentrate
10 lbs fresh damsons or sloes
1¼ pint red rose petals
5 lbs honey
yeast nutrient
Grey Owl Pommard Yeast
Campden tablets
pectozyme

Remove the stones from the sloes or damsons and put in a plastic bucket. Add 1 lb honey and a gallon of boiling water, stir well and leave for forty-eight hours. Stir frequently, crushing the fruit with a wooden spoon. Add pectozyme as soon as the liquid is cool.

After forty-eight hours, add yeast, put bucket in warm place and ferment for five days. Add rose petals on second day. Stir frequently.

(This is called 'fermenting on pulp' and the process extracts the maximum flavour, colour and goodness from the fruit. The reason for doing it ahead of the main fermentation is because it simplifies the straining operation. When the wine is put in the oak cask for maturing, it is important that none of the pulp should go too; and obviously it is easier to strain, thoroughly, a gallon of liquid from a bucket as opposed to four and a half gallons from a much larger container.)

When the pulp has fermented for five days, begin the main operation. Take a large plastic container, for instance a dustbin, and put in the grape concentrate and 1 lb honey. Add a gallon of hot water and stir well.

Now take the bucket with the pulp fermentation and siphon the contents into a second bucket, leaving behind as much as possible of the residue at the bottom.

Cover the top of the main container with a large piece of material – either linen, nylon or terylene. Tie it firmly in place with string, but allow to sag a little in the middle. Strain the contents of bucket through it.

Remove the filter material and make up the liquid in the container to five gallons.

Add yeast, cover and leave to ferment. As mentioned earlier, the temperature does not have to be so warm when larger amounts are being fermented; but it should certainly be no colder than the low sixties.

Check the progress of fermentation with a hydrometer (see page 97) and feed in the remaining 3 lbs honey in small regular doses. Add a teaspoonful of yeast nutrient with the honey every now and then, perhaps three or four times in all.

When the fermentation is over and the liquid has begun to clear, siphon it into an oak cask. By this time the liquid will have reduced from 5 gallons to about 4½ – the right amount for the cask. Add 5 Campden tablets.

Leave the cask in a cool even temperature and rack the wine every three months. This can be done by siphoning it back into a fermentation container, rinsing out the cask thoroughly with cold water, then returning the wine. Top up with a dry white wine. Add 5 Campden tablets every other racking.

There are no hard and fast rules about the length of time that claret should remain in the cask, but three years is probably the minimum. Taste a little every time you rack and notice how the harsh tannin flavour begins to soften and mellow. When you feel that the wine has really become drinkable, this is the time to bottle. (Wine dislikes light, so use dark bottles – amber or green.)

Store the bottles in a cool dark place for at least a year, preferably two.

It may well continue to improve for many years thereafter, but we're not immortal, are we?

Liebfraumilch

      7 cans Liebfraumilch Concentrate
      10 lbs cooking apples
      5 lbs white grapes
      5 lbs sugar
      5 lbs honey
      $1\frac{1}{4}$ pint white or yellow rose petals
      yeast nutrient
      Liebfraumilch yeast
      Campden tablets

Chop the apples, put in a big saucepan or preserving pan, cover with water and bring to the boil. Simmer gently for half an hour.

Add the fresh grapes and leave for forty-eight hours. Stir repeatedly, mashing and pounding the fruit with a big wooden spoon.

Transfer the pulp and liquid to a plastic bucket, add 1 lb sugar and make up to a gallon. Stir vigorously. Add the yeast, put the covered bucket in a warm place and ferment 'on pulp' (see page 132) for five days, stirring daily. Add the rose petals on the second day.

Now take a large plastic container, put in the grape concentrate and 2 lbs sugar, add a gallon of hot water and stir well. Strain on the liquid from the pulp fermentation, as described in Claret recipe, and make up to five and a half gallons.

Add the yeast and keep the container in a warm place for twenty-four hours when fermentation should be well under way. Then transfer to cooler temperature, 60°F or even a little below.

Fermentation should be slow and gentle, and could take several weeks. Check progress with a hydrometer, as for claret, and add the remaining sugar and honey in gradual doses. Add a teaspoonful of nutrient on three or four occasions.

When fermentation is over, siphon into five glass gallon jars, or one 5-gallon carboy. Remember that white wine should be exposed to the air as little as possible, so be sure to keep each jar full. Add one Campden tablet per gallon and fit with an airlock.

Store the jars in a cool dark place. (Sunlight should be avoided like the plague.)

As white wines dislike oxidation, racking should not be carried out as frequently as with red wines. Rack into clean jars after four months, adding one Campden tablet per gallon, then leave for six months.

The wine is now ready for bottling. You may find that it is extremely drinkable after another four to six months; but it will probably continue to develop and improve for at least another year. Unlike claret, this wine is unlikely to improve if kept longer than two or three years.

Champagne

2 cans Champagne Concentrate (to make two gallons)
4 lbs fresh green gooseberries
1 pint Schloer apple juice
8 oz sugar
2 lbs honey
yeast nutrient
champagne yeast
Campden tablets
pectozyme

Top and tail the gooseberries and put in a bucket with 8 oz sugar. Cover with warm water and, when this has cooled, add pectozyme. Leave for twenty-four hours. Make up to a gallon with blood-heat water, add the yeast and ferment 'on pulp' (see page 132).

Put the Champagne Concentrate in a 2½ gallon, or larger, plastic container, strain on liquid from the pulp fermentation, make up to 2 gallons and proceed in the usual way. Try to keep the temperature in the mid-sixties. Add the apple juice after a few days.

Keep a careful check with the hydrometer, and when all the honey has been fed in and the reading is down to 1·005, prepare to bottle.

The wine should be put in champagne bottles, corked and wired, and kept for about a week at a slightly warmer temperature, up to 70°F. This is to encourage the secondary fermentation to get under way in the bottles.

After a week or so, move the bottles to a colder temperature, around 50°F. Store them horizontally, with corks tilting downwards; and for the first ten days, turn each bottle every day – just a slight but sharp twist to left and right.

Yeast sediment will now begin to settle on the cork and this has to be removed, which is rather a tricky operation. Allow the bottles to remain undisturbed for about six months, then take out of doors.

Hold each bottle with the head pointing downwards, remove the fastening and ease out the cork. It should come out explosively, carrying the accumulation of yeast in the neck of the bottle with it. Quickly turn the bottle upright and place your hand over the top to prevent any further escape of gas or liquid. When the effervescence dies down, remove any remaining traces of yeast from bottle neck with your finger, and add a small glass of brandy (for a dry champagne) or a small quantity of sugar syrup (for a sweeter champagne).

Re-cork and wire the bottles and return to storage. They should now be placed horizontally, without any downward tilt of the head, and left for at least a year before drinking.

☐ *This is a bit of a performance but the real champagne lover will find it worthwhile.*

Port

Follow either of the two recipes given for port in Chapter 9. The only difference is that the wine should be matured in wood for two years and racked at four-monthly intervals. Keep for a further year in bottles.

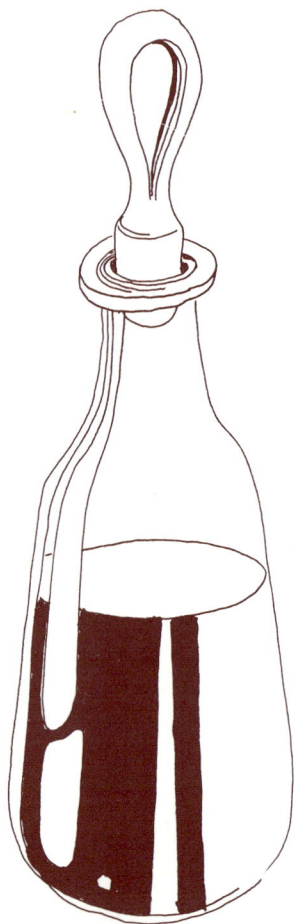

12. Home Brewing

Home Brewing

There is far less prejudice against homemade beers than against homemade wines. In fact, as with cakes and jam, your own make is even expected to be better than anything you can buy.

It's certainly a fact that beer is gloriously easy to make and gloriously quick to mature. Both taste and strength can have real guts, and the economy is even more dazzling than with wine – sometimes amounting to as little as a fifth of the commercial price. It's also very easy to vary the type and make it strong or mild, robust or delicate, dark or pale. Whatever your taste, there should be no problem at all in suiting it.

A caution
Initially, many home brewers like the idea of making a strong beer, looking on the strength as a sign of quality. But if you also look on it as a long, thirst-quenching drink, this approach can have its drawbacks. Always remember that beer can be brought up to a 9% alcoholic content, which is as strong as claret; and you wouldn't expect to drink two or three pints of claret without feeling the punch, not to mention the hangover. (There are those who say that hangovers from strong beers and ciders are among the worst in the world.) So if you do decide to make a strong brew, it's only sense to drink it like wine rather than beer.

As with wine, the alcoholic content is determined by the amount of sugar you use. The more malt you begin with, the more sugar you add, the stronger the beer will be. You can reckon that 1 lb malt extract plus 2 lbs added sugar will create a gallon of super-strong beer with an alcoholic content nudging 10%. 1 lb malt extract plus ½ lb added sugar will be medium strength, somewhere between 5% and 6% alcohol. ½ lb malt extract plus ½ lb sugar will be mild, perhaps as low as 3%.

Basically, there are three ways to brew beer:

1. Using the beer kits, now available at many chemists and all winemaking stores.

2. Using malt

3. Using malt extract

The beer kits, like the wine kits, are the quickest and easiest operation. They usually involve nothing more strenuous than the addition of water, sugar and yeast; and the results are extremely good. Unican, Tom Caxton, Geordie, produce excellent bitters, lagers and stouts, and they can really be recommended to anyone who wants to play safe and is not too interested in experimenting.

The other two methods are a question of recipes, i.e. you put together your own ingredients rather than taking a ready-made combination. You get more variety in flavour and in strength, you can suit your own taste better, and they usually work out more economically. If this appeals to you, it's all much more fun – just as it's more fun to follow cooking recipes rather than to open tins. But one must, of course, accept that it is also harder work.

The second method – using malt – is the traditional one, and is still used by commercial brewers. It is generally accepted that this is the way to make the best and truest beers, but one must admit that it is rather too troublesome and difficult for most home brewers. Malt comes in the form of whole grains, and it cannot be used as it stands. The starch must first be converted into sugar, and this sugar extracted by a process called 'mashing'.
First, the malt grains have to be cracked. (This part isn't too difficult: a coffee grinder is ideal, but a rolling pin will do the job.) The cracked grains must then be soaked in hot water, at 130°F, for at least eight hours. This isn't so easy because the 130°F must be maintained at the same level throughout. Next, the liquid must be strained and boiled up with the hops for an hour; and again, this isn't so easy if you want to make four or five gallons at a time.
I may add that this is the simplest possible way to 'mash'. There are other far more complicated and laborious procedures!

The real disadvantage, apart from the time and trouble, is the initial investment. You can't really manage without an immersion heater (page 30) to maintain the temperature at 130°F, and a Burco boiler or equivalent is needed for the final boil-up.

With malt extract, the work has been done for you. The sugar has been extracted from the starch and is ready to go to work; so all you have to do is add the yeast, hops, sugar and any other ingredients. As with grape concentrate versus fresh grapes, it is a compromise; but most people would agree that the malt extracts now available deserve almost unqualified praise. A few years ago, there was very little choice, and anyone asking at the chemist for malt extract was liable to go off with something tasting strongly of cod-liver oil. But nowadays, malt extract is made to such a high standard that even commercial brewers have been known to use it when the barley crop is poor. It is said that it gives a rather nutty flavour to the beer, but few of the home brewers I have consulted with have noticed, still less objected.
There are, however, beer makers who like to experiment, so I have included recipes which use part extract and part whole malt grains. In this combination, the mashing can be simplified and the results are certainly very good. Anyone who would like to go still further and mash in the traditional way should read C. J. Berry's *Home-Brewed Beers and Stouts*.

Cider

I have not found a satisfactory answer to cider making. You can extract the juice from the apples yourself, using either an electric juicer or a cider press. Unfortunately, both these items are expensive, and the latter is also bulky and messy. You can also buy apple concentrate, but the price of your cider will then work out almost as expensive as a homemade wine. I have tried commercial cider kits, and didn't find the result very agreeable. It was extraordinarily slow to ferment, and the taste left much to be desired.
I have, however, included one recipe which seemed to work quite well, using fresh apples, and not calling for electric juicers or cider presses. If your interest in this chapter is in cider rather than beer turn immediately to page 150.

Medium Bitter

1 lb malt extract
1 oz dried hops
½ lb demerara sugar
1 teaspoonful granulated dried yeast nutrient

The cans of malt extract should be treated like cans of grape concentrate and *thoroughly warmed* in advance. And it pays to activate the beer yeast a few hours before use, just as it pays to activate the wine yeast.

Pour the malt extract into a plastic bucket, add the sugar and a quart of hot water. Stir well till all is dissolved. Put the hops, except for one good handful, into a nylon stocking and tie a knot at the top. Put the stocking into a saucepan with a quart of boiling water and simmer for ten minutes. Add this liquid to the bucket. Repeat the process twice more, boiling the hop-filled stocking in a fresh quart of water. (When making beer in larger quantities – say, four or five gallons – boil up hops with a gallon of water at a time instead of a quart.) Put the remaining handful of hops into another nylon stocking, tie in the same way and float in bucket.

When the liquid has cooled to blood-heat, add yeast and a teaspoonful of yeast nutrient. Cover bucket and leave in warm place – around 70°F – for a week. Fermentation will be violent for the first few days; and it will stop more suddenly and completely than a wine fermentation. Ideally, you should check with a hydrometer to see that the reading is down to 1·005. (If too much sugar remains in the liquid, the fermentation in the bottle might become too violent and shatter the glass.) One can get a stuck fermentation with beer as with wine; but this can usually be cured by pouring liquid into another container, stirring vigorously and adding a little more yeast. The problem is very unlikely to occur if the temperature is right.

Fermentation is almost certain to be over in a week, and now is the time to bottle and 'prime'. Siphon the liquid into screw-top bottles or into beer bottles that can be sealed with plastic caps (available at

Boots). Ordinary bottles with corks won't do, because the corks will simply blow out. Don't fill the bottles too full: leave an inch or two of air space. 'Priming' means a last minute addition of castor sugar before the bottles are sealed. Add a level teaspoonful per pint – no more.

Store the bottles in a cool place for two weeks after which they should be ready for drinking.

There's bound to be a certain amount of sediment at the bottom of each bottle; so when you pour, *never tilt the bottle back* – keep on pouring into the appropriate number of glasses until you can see you are reaching the dregs.

☐ *This is one of the most successful beers I have tried – by which I mean that almost everyone seems to like it. There is noticeably more flavour than in a commercial brand but it is still quite light. Its nearest relation is perhaps Double Diamond.*

Strong Bitter

1 lb malt extract
1 oz dried hops
1 lb brown sugar (raw Barbados is best)
pinch of salt
1 small lemon (or half a large one)
4 tablespoonfuls cold tea
yeast and nutrient

Follow procedure described in first recipe (page 143).
Add a pinch of salt to the first quart of water in which the hops are boiled up. Add the juice of a lemon and the cold tea to the bucket once the liquid has been made up to a gallon.

☐*If you want something that packs a fair punch, both in punch and flavour, this is superb.*

Mild Bitter

1 lb malt extract
$\frac{3}{4}$ oz dried hops
yeast and nutrient

Follow procedure described in first recipe (page 143).

☐ *This is lighter in flavour and can be drunk, safely and pleasurably, by the pint – or even the quart.*

Brown Ale

1 lb malt extract
2 oz black malt grains
1 oz dried hops
$\frac{1}{2}$ lb brown sugar
yeast and nutrient

Put the extract and the black malt grains in a large saucepan, add 5 pints of boiling water and simmer for half an hour. Add the hops tied in a nylon stocking and simmer for a further ten minutes.

Strain the liquid into plastic bucket and stir in the sugar.

Now proceed as in first recipe (page 143), boiling up two further quarts of water with the hops in their stocking.

☐ *As this recipe includes whole malt, the method is slightly different.*

Milk Stout

1 lb malt extract
4 oz black malt grains
4 oz lactose
2 oz flaked barley
1 lb brown sugar
yeast and nutrient
$1\frac{1}{2}$ oz dried hops

The method is the same as for Brown Ale (page 146). The flaked barley should be simmered for half an hour with the malt extract and malt grains. Add the lactose with the sugar. Traditionally, stout should be made with soft or very soft water. If you live in a hard water district, you can buy a 'softening' treatment from winemaking stores. One teaspoonful of salt per four gallons of water also helps.

☐ *Very smooth and nourishing and good for you.*

Stout

Same recipe as for Milk Stout, but omitting the lactose.

Cock Ale

1 lb malt extract
1 oz dried hops
$\frac{1}{2}$ lb demerara sugar
yeast and nutrient
pieces of cooked chicken and chicken bones
(about a tenth of a bird)
$\frac{1}{2}$ lb raisins
pinch of mace
2 cloves
1 bottle strong white wine
(you can use your own white Vin Ordinaire – page 46 –
strengthened with a little brandy)

Crush or grind the chicken bones as finely as you can and put them in a bowl with the pieces of cooked chicken, raisins, mace and cloves. Soak for twenty-four hours in the strong white wine.

Make a gallon of Medium Bitter (page 143) and when it is fermenting hard, add the contents of the bowl. Leave to ferment a week longer than usual and mature for at least a month in the bottle.

☐ *This is an old English recipe, rather exotic and extravagant. It produces a very strong flavoured brew of the barley wine type, and should be drunk in a wine, rather than a beer, size of glass.*

Lager

1 lb malt extract
1 lb pale malt
$\frac{1}{2}$ lb sugar
1 oz dried hops
yeast and nutrient

The same method as for Brown Ale (page 146).

☐*Refreshingly light, with a clean crisp taste. Should be served cold.*

Cider

4 lbs apples
(a mixture is best – mostly cookers but with a few
eating apples and even crab apples included)
1 lb sugar
2 lemons
yeast

Chop apples in small pieces, cores and all, and put them through a mincer.

Put the pulp in a large bowl and pour on six quarts of cold water. Leave for a week or so, stirring well each day.

Strain the liquid into a bucket, stir in the lemon juice and sugar and yeast, cover and leave to ferment.

When fermentation is over, bottle in screw-top cider or beer bottles. Cider takes longer than beer to mature and is best left for a few months.

This recipe makes a medium dry cider. A sweet one will need 2 lbs sugar.

☐*For this one really needs an apple press or a juice extractor. If you have neither, a certain amount of work is involved but the cider addict may find it worth while.*

13. Cooking with Wine

Cooking with Wine

Cook-books, old and new, have always extolled the virtues of cooking with wine; and you won't need to be told that red wine improves the flavour of red meat, that white wine can do beautiful things to fish, that liqueurs have a way with fruit, and so on and so forth. The more standard recipes, however, tend to assume that only expensive in-gredients deserve the added luxury of wine – and this chapter will take exactly the opposite point of view.

In these days of rapidly rising costs, we are more and more thrown back on the cheaper cuts of meat, the less exotic fish, and the not-so-fancy puddings. At the same time, our cooking standards are rising (the English housewife has even learned how to cook cabbage) and we are not in the least prepared to accept that restricted budgets mean horrible meals. An enormous amount of skill and ingenuity has in fact gone into the exploration of low-cost recipes which contrive to taste expensive.

Of all ingredients, wine is perhaps the most brilliant at transforming a mundane flavour. It is hardly realistic to suggest its constant use when the commercial price is going through the roof – any economy on meat or fish might be rapidly cancelled out. But you can score spectacularly if you have made the wine yourself.

The economy is marvellous enough when you use your own daily grape wine at around 15p a bottle; but you can do even better than this. Cooking wine can be made very successfully with ingredients like blackcurrant syrup, parsnips, elderberries, elderflowers, dried fruits – *and no grape at all*. No, I haven't forgotten all the things I said about their unfamiliar and unacceptable flavours as table wines; but their effect in cooking is an altogether different affair. For example, I would defy anyone to distinguish – let alone prefer – a jugged hare made with elderberry wine from a jugged hare made with burgundy, or a jelly made with elderflower wine from a jelly made with hock.

This is particularly satisfying when you realise that the cost of a gallon of an elderberry or elderflower wine, if you pick the fruit and flowers yourself, is hardly more than the cost of 3 lbs sugar – and no one can complain about that.

I have included recipes for these cooking wines at the start of this chapter. You may consider them an unnecessary effort in view of the cheapness of the basic grape concentrate wines; but if you really enjoy wine in your recipes, and plan to be lavish about it, I think they are well worth consideration.

All the food recipes are simple and inexpensive. They assume that you only have a limited amount of time to spend in the kitchen, and that the cleverest thing in the world is to produce a good meal fast.

They will serve about four people.

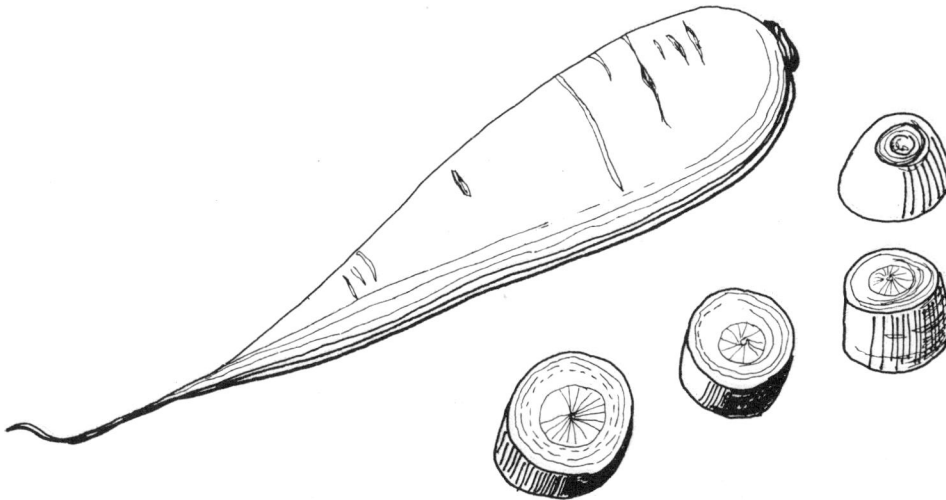

Elderberry Cooking Wine

4 lbs elderberries
3½ lbs sugar
wine yeast
nutrient
½ oz citric acid

Strip the berries from the stalks, and put in a plastic bucket. Pound and mash with a wooden spoon. Add sugar, cover with boiling water, stir well, and leave until cool. Make up to a gallon with blood-heat water, add the citric acid and activated yeast and proceed in the usual way – i.e. leave to ferment in warm place for about eight days, adding yeast nutrient around third day. Strain into a gallon jar, plug with cotton wool and leave at room temperature for three or four weeks, when it will be ready for cooking use.

☐ *This is a strong flavoured wine which will taste pretty harsh in its young days. It is, however, excellent in recipes like casseroles or jugged hare where a substantial red wine is called for. Sweetened with sugar, it can also stand in for port.*

Elderflower Cooking Wine

1 pint elderflowers (loosely packed)
1 oz whole ginger
1 orange
1 lemon
3 lbs sugar
wine yeast
nutrient

Choose the elderflower blossoms carefully, rejecting anything that looks jaded or overblown. The young, just-opening ones are best. Wash in cold water, leave to dry, then measure in a pint jug.

Put the elderflowers and ginger in a bucket with the sugar, cover with boiling water and stir well. Leave until cool. Add the juice of the orange and lemon, make up to a gallon with blood-heat water and proceed as usual.

☐*Like elderberry, this can have quite a pungent flavour. A very useful white wine.*

Blackcurrant Cooking Wine

12 oz bottle Ribena (or other blackcurrant cordial)
3 lemons
3 lbs sugar
wine yeast
nutrient

Put Ribena and sugar in a bucket with about a quart of boiling water, and stir well. Leave to cool, make up to a gallon with blood-heat water, add lemon juice and activated yeast, and proceed in usual way.

☐ *If elderberries aren't in season (or you don't want to pick them anyway) try this recipe for a robust red wine.*

Orange and Rosehip Cooking Wine

10 oranges
12 oz bottle Rosehip syrup
2 lbs sugar
half cupful strong tea
wine yeast
nutrient

Put the juice from the oranges, the Rosehip syrup and the sugar in a bucket, cover with warm water and stir well. Add the tea, make up to a gallon and proceed as usual.

☐*This is a non-seasonal white wine with rather less flavour.*

Rosé

2 lbs mixed dried fruit
1 pint can of orange juice
2 lemons
6 oz Ribena (or similar blackcurrant cordial)
2 lbs sugar
wine yeast
nutrient

Put dried fruit and sugar in a bucket, cover with boiling water and stir well. Allow to cool. Add orange juice, juice from lemons and Ribena, make up to a gallon and proceed as usual.

☐ *It is not really necessary to have a cooking rosé because you can always blend your red and white to an appropriate colour. However, this recipe is so good and so easy, I couldn't resist putting it in.*

Potato and Salami Soup

1 lb potatoes
1 large onion
(or if available, 12 spring onions)
4 rashers bacon (chopped)
6 slices salami (chopped)
½ pint dry white wine
thyme
seasoning
butter

Peel the potatoes and cut in thin strips. Sauté the onion in butter, (if you are using spring onions, include some of the green parts) in a saucepan, and then add the potato strips and 1½ pints boiling water. Season to taste with salt, pepper and a little thyme, and simmer for twenty minutes.
Fry the chopped bacon and salami together and add them to the soup with the white wine. Simmer a few minutes longer, then decorate with parsley and serve.

☐ *This is good and filling, and can even be used as the main dish for occasions like Sunday suppers.*

Chicken Liver Pâté

$\frac{1}{2}$ lb chicken livers
$\frac{1}{4}$ pint cream
$\frac{1}{2}$ clove garlic
3 tablespoons red wine
1 oz butter
seasoning

Cook the livers in butter; then put in the blender or through the mincer. Season with salt and pepper, and stir in the crushed garlic and the red wine. Whip the cream and fold it in. Chill in the refrigerator before serving.

☐ *This is rich but light.*

Tuna Salad

1 tin Tuna fish (7 oz)
mayonnaise (made with 2 egg yolks and olive oil)
$\frac{1}{2}$ clove garlic
4 tablespoons white wine
lettuce
stuffed olives
seasoning

Make the mayonnaise in the usual way, stirring the olive oil drop by drop into the egg yolks. Season well with salt and freshly-ground pepper, and stir in the crushed garlic.
Drain the tuna and mash with the wine. Then mix with the mayonnaise. Serve on crisp lettuce leaves, and decorate with stuffed olives.

☐ *If you are in a hurry, use bought mayonnaise; but your own will be very much better.*

Moules Marinière

2 pints mussels
12 spring onions (or 1 large onion)
½ pint white wine
2 oz butter
chopped parsley
pepper

Clean the mussels thoroughly in cold water, discarding any that are beginning to open. Put the butter and chopped onion into a large saucepan and fry gently. (If using spring onions, add plenty of the green parts.) Season with freshly-ground pepper, and pour in the wine. When all is bubbling, add the mussels, put the lid on the saucepan, turn up the heat and cook for at least five minutes, shaking the pan at intervals. When the mussels have opened, they are ready.
Serve in a large dish with all the liquid, and sprinkle with chopped parsley.

☐ *This dish always impresses people as exotic, but in fact the ingredients are very economical. Look carefully at the mussels before you buy them to make sure they are closed: any that are beginning to open are not fresh and will have to be thrown out.*

Gazpacho

1½ lbs tomatoes (the riper the better)
1 onion
1 green pepper
1 clove garlic
1 slice brown bread
1 tablespoonful olive oil
½ pint rosé wine
juice of 1 lemon
seasoning

Except for the lemon juice and seasoning, all the ingredients are put in the blender. The tomatoes should be skinned and their pips removed, the pepper sliced and its seeds removed, the onion peeled and sliced, and the crusts cut off the bread. When blended, season with salt and lemon juice. Chill in the refrigerator, and serve in bowls with a cube of ice in each.

Oyster Dip

2 oz double cream cheese
mayonnaise (your own, if possible)
2 tablespoons white wine
A 4–5 oz jar of smoked oysters
Half a cupful of ripe olives
Lemon juice
Seasoning

Mash the cream cheese with the wine. Then mix in enough mayonnaise to get a smooth, creamy-thick consistency.
Add the oysters (chopped) and the olives (minced) and season with salt, pepper and lemon juice. Serve with biscuits.

☐ *This is useful for parties. It is also very nice to have with an everyday pre-dinner cocktail.*

Beef Casserole

       1 lb stewing steak in one piece
       1 large onion (or four sliced leeks)
       a few carrots
       1 packet dried onion soup mix
       1 clove garlic
       red wine
       seasoning

Put the steak in one piece in a casserole dish, and cover with sliced onions (or leeks) carrots and crushed garlic. Season with salt and pepper. Sprinkle the soup mix all over, then pour on enough wine to cover. Cook in a very low oven for two and half hours.

☐ *Quite possibly, this is the easiest casserole in the world.*

Sausages au Vin

       2 lbs pork sausages
       2 tomatoes
       2 onions
       $1\frac{1}{2}$ oz butter
       $\frac{1}{2}$ pint white wine
       2 teaspoonfuls flour

Grill the sausages until browned. Fry the sliced onions and butter in a pan until golden, add the tomatoes (skinned and chopped) and the sausages. Pour on the wine, stir in flour, season well, and cook for about 20 minutes, stirring occasionally and turning the sausages.

☐ *Try and get some really good pork sausages for this dish.*

Jugged Hare

marinade
(made with 1 pint red wine, 2 tablespoonfuls salad oil, a sliced
shallot, 2 bay leaves, pepper)

1 hare
(cut into manageable pieces)
1 tablespoonful beurre manie
(an equal quantity of flour and butter mixed together)
1 large onion stuck with two cloves
1 stick of celery
2 carrots
8 peppercorns
2 tablespoonfuls bacon fat
flour
seasoning
1 tablespoonful redcurrant jelly
red wine

Put the ingredients for the marinade into a saucepan, bring to the
boil, and allow to cool. Soak the pieces of hare in this marinade for
several hours.

Dry well, cover with flour, and brown quickly in bacon fat, using a
flameproof casserole. Add the onion, cut in half, the sliced celery and
carrots, and peppercorns, and cover with red wine and a little water.
Season, and cook in low oven for about three hours.

Remove the pieces of hare to a dish. Make a smooth, thick sauce with
strained liquid from the casserole and the beurre manie. Stir in the
redcurrant jelly (or if you have any homemade port, use a wineglassful

instead). Pour the sauce over the pieces of hare, and stand in a medium oven (Reg 4, 350°) for ten or fifteen minutes and serve very hot.

☐*This dish does involve a certain amount of preparation, and not everyone likes the very strong, game-y flavour. However, if you do like game and can't afford the traditional birds, jugged hare is a magnificent alternative.*

Kedgeree on Wine Rice

1 lb cod
$\frac{1}{2}$ lb salmon (frozen will do)
4 eggs
4 oz butter
$\frac{1}{4}$ pint cream (whipped)
white wine
8 oz rice
seasoning

Cook the rice in the oven, substituting wine for water. See that it is well drained and dried.
Poach the fish in water, then remove the skin and bones. Hardboil the eggs at the same time.

Mix the rice, fish and chopped eggs in a bowl over a saucepan of very hot water. Blend in the butter, and season well. Fold in the whipped cream, and serve immediately.

☐*Instead of cooking the fish in wine, in the usual way, this recipe cooks the rice in wine instead of water.*

Kidneys with Wine Gravy

4 lambs' kidneys
3 cloves garlic
juice of half a lemon
cooking oil
stock or water
red wine
seasoning

Fry the chopped kidneys in very hot oil to which crushed garlic has been added. Add lemon juice and seasoning.
Make a gravy with the juices from the frying pan and water. Shortly before serving, add two tablespoonfuls of red wine and pour over the kidneys. Serve on rice.

☐ *When the wine is added to the gravy shortly before serving, the flavour comes through strongly.*

Marinated Hamburgers

marinade
(made with 1 pint red wine, 1 crushed clove garlic, and two tablespoonfuls salad oil)

1 lb mince
seasoning

Marinate the mince overnight. Drain, squeeze out the liquid, and dry a little in very low oven. Season to taste, make up into patties, and fry or grill in the usual way.

Wine Jelly

$\frac{3}{4}$ pint white wine
2 tablespoonfuls lemon juice
2 tablespoonfuls orange juice
$\frac{3}{4}$ oz gelatine
4 oz castor sugar

Dissolve the sugar in $\frac{1}{2}$ pint of boiling water. Cool the liquid a little and sprinkle in the gelatine. When it has melted, add the wine and fruit juices. Strain into a jelly mould and chill in the refrigerator. Serve with or without whipped cream.

☐ *This is a most acceptable dessert to follow a rich main course. It also tastes delicious made with a rosé wine.*

Simple Peach

six fresh peaches
2 tablespoonfuls lemon juice
4 tablespoonfuls white wine
sugar to taste

Skin and slice the peaches, removing the stones. Add lemon juice and wine. You can sweeten the wine with a little sugar if desired.

☐ *An absurdly simple dish that almost everyone likes.*

Apple Crumble

1½ lbs cooking apples
¼ pint white wine (with sugar to taste)
2 oz soft brown sugar
2 oz butter
4 oz plain flour
pinch of cinnamon

Peel and core the apples, put in a casserole with the white wine
sweetened to taste. Cover, and heat in low oven for half an hour.
Rub the flour, butter, sugar and cinnamon together into a bread-
crumby mixture. Sprinkle this over the fruit, and turn the oven up to
Reg. 6/400°. Put the dish, uncovered, in the oven and cook for about
20 minutes, or until crumble mixture is golden brown.

☐*Rather more filling, and extremely popular with children.*

Strawberry Cream Shortcake

1 packet shortcake biscuits
3 oz butter
$\frac{3}{4}$ pint rosé wine, sweetened to taste
1 packet gelatine
$\frac{1}{4}$ pint double cream
1 lb fresh strawberries (or frozen)

Melt the gelatine in the warmed wine. Put the biscuits in the blender, or crush with rolling pin, and mix with the creamed butter. Put in a flan dish and cool in the refrigerator.
Whip the cream, and fold in the strawberries and the mixture of wine and gelatine. Pour this on to flan base and leave to set.
Decorate with a few extra strawberries.

☐*Not at all slimming, but extremely good.*

Chocolate Cream

4 tablespoonfuls Cadbury's (or similar) Drinking Chocolate
2 egg whites
1 pint cream
2 tablespoonfuls Poor Man's Brandy (page 118)

Just whisk all this up together until the texture is suitably light and creamy. Serve with wafer biscuits.

☐*As simple as the peach, but a good deal richer.*

Sherry Ice Cream

4 eggs (separated)
4 oz icing sugar (sifted)
½ pint double cream (whipped)
sherry (and brandy) to taste

Whisk egg yolks with wire whisk in a small bowl until well blended. Whisk egg whites with rotary whisk in another bowl. (If you *can* afford a copper bowl, the difference is amazing.) Blend in icing sugar, gradually. Slowly combine egg yolks and meringue mixture, and fold in whipped cream. Add sherry and brandy to taste, and put in deep freeze.

☐ *You can cheat and use a bought vanilla ice cream. In this case, you simply allow it to soften and stir in your own sherry to taste, strengthened – if you can afford it – with a little brandy. Chill in deep freeze. A home-made ice cream will, however, taste incomparably better; and this recipe is a real joy.*

14. Let's End with a Party

Let's End with a Party

This is the chapter that needs no introduction. All that need be said is that, when you make your own ingredients, you can afford a party every day – and twice on Sundays! First, for winter parties:

Mistletoe Mull

    1 bottle burgundy (page 61)
    2 lemons
    1 cup granulated sugar
    4 cloves (or $\frac{3}{4}$ teaspoonful ground cinnamon)
    2 cups water

Boil the water with the sugar, cinnamon and cloves for five minutes. Add the thinly sliced lemons and allow to stand for ten minutes. Add wine and heat slowly, but do not allow to boil. Put in a large jug, and serve very hot.

The Bishop

1½ bottles Port (page 108)
4 cloves
2 oz lump sugar
2 lemons
mixed spices
1 pint water

Stick one of the lemons with cloves and put in a medium oven for half
an hour. Put the port into a saucepan and bring almost to the boil.
In another saucepan, boil 1 pint water, adding a good pinch of mixed
spices and the lemon stuck with cloves. Pour this liquid into the port,
discarding the first lemon. Rub the lump sugar on the rind of the second
lemon and put the lemony lumps into a big jug. Add half the juice of
the second lemon. Now pour in the hot wine, stir, and serve.

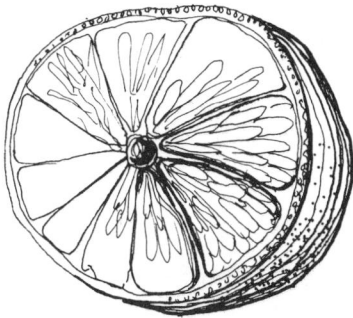

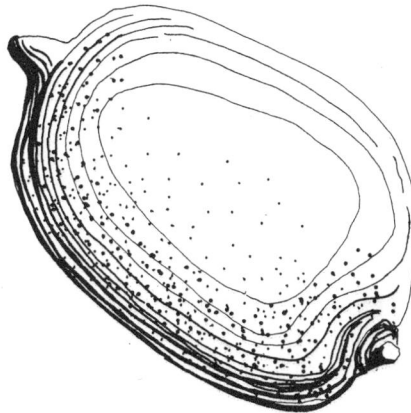

Beer and Brandy Punch

2 pints strong beer (page 145)
1 pint Poor Man's Brandy (page 118)
1 thinly pared rind of lemon
4 oz sugar
1 pint water
grated nutmeg

Put all the ingredients into a saucepan and bring to the boil. Remove from the heat immediately and pour into punch bowl or jug. Sprinkle with grated nutmeg and serve at once.

Cherry Punch

1 bottle red wine (page 61)
2 lbs ripe black cherries
2 lemons
3 oz sugar

Remove the stones from the cherries over a saucepan so no juice is wasted. Add the pared rind of the lemons, the sugar and water to the saucepan and simmer for about ten minutes. Remove the lemon rind, add the wine and cherries and heat gently. Serve very hot.

Christmas Cordial

1 bottle red wine
4 oz (eight tablespoonfuls) Ribena
juice of two lemons
stick of cinnamon
1 pint water

Blend the ingredients together, and simmer gently for fifteen minutes.
Serve hot, and sprinkle with a little grated nutmeg if desired.

Sherry Shiver

1 bottle sherry (dry) (page 104)
1 pint ginger beer (page 179)
Juice of 1 lemon
Juice of 1 orange

Chill the sherry and ginger beer in the refrigerator for several hours.
Put the ice cubes in a jug, pour in the sherry and ginger beer and fruit
juice. Serve immediately.

Champagne Cup

3 pints champagne (page 81)
½ pint Poor Man's Brandy (page 118)
2 oranges (rind and juice)
2 lemons (rind and juice)
3 oz sugar

Boil the orange and lemon rinds with sugar in ½ pint water for about 5 minutes. Strain into a jug or bowl and add the fruit juices, champagne and brandy, and as many ice cubes as are needed to chill.

Gin Fizz

1 bottle Poor Man's Gin (page 115)
4 tablespoonfuls lemon juice
4 egg whites (whipped)
sugar to taste
soda water

Blend the ingredients together in a jug, and add sugar and soda to taste.

Dubonnet Cocktail

1 bottle Poor Man's Gin (page 115)
1 bottle 'Cheat' Dubonnet (page 110)
3 lemons (sliced)
soda water

Mix the gin and Dubonnet together. Add sliced lemons and soda to taste, with ice.

Strawberry Fare

1 bottle of rosé wine
1 lb strawberries
2 oz sugar
2 8-oz bottles Schweppes Bitter Lemon
a few slices of cucumber

Slice the strawberries, keeping back a few for decoration, cover with the sugar and soak in a little rosé wine for an hour or two.
Add the other ingredients, decorate with sliced cucumber and remaining strawberries, and serve very cold.

☐ *This recipe and the three which follow are not completely un-alcoholic, but they are very light and can be drunk, harmlessly, in large quantities.*

Summer Spice

1 bottle white wine
stick of cinnamon
3 cloves
pinch of ground nutmeg
grated rind of 1 orange
$\frac{1}{4}$ pint lemon squash
$\frac{1}{4}$ pint orange squash
soda water to taste

Mix the cinnamon, cloves, nutmeg and orange rind in the lemon and orange squash, and simmer for 10 minutes.
Strain carefully, add the white wine and serve very cold with soda water to taste. A decoration of fresh mint is nice.

Ginger Beer

1 oz root ginger,
1 lb sugar
1 gallon of water
2 lemons
$\frac{1}{4}$ oz cream of tartar
1 teaspoonful beer yeast
1 gallon water

Crush the root ginger and put in a bowl with the sugar and cream of tartar. Pour on boiling gallon of water and stir well.
Peel the lemons, stripping off every particle of white pith, then cut them into thin slices and add to the bowl.
Cover bowl with cloth, and when liquid is cool, sprinkle on the yeast. Leave for two days.
Skim the yeast off the surface, strain off the lemon and ginger, and bottle in sturdy screw-top bottles. Will be ready in three days.

Orange Sun

1 bottle white wine
1 pint orange juice (fresh or frozen)
½ pint pineapple juice
juice of 2 lemons
a few slices of fresh apple and orange

Blend the fruit juices with the wine and chill thoroughly.
Serve with crushed ice, and decorate with slices of fresh apple and orange.

Pink Peach

1 bottle rosé (see page 67)
1 bottle Sauternes (page 79)
1 wineglassful Peach Liqueur (page 119)
1 pint soda water
1 fresh peach, sliced

Put the cubes of ice in a bowl and pour on rosé wine. Add the sliced peach, Sauternes and Peach Liqueur. Leave in the refrigerator for at least half an hour and add the soda water immediately before serving.

Black Beauty

Non-alcoholic

> 6 tablespoonfuls blackberry juice
> (strained from can of blackberries)
> 6 tablespoonfuls Ribena
> juice of four lemons
> 1 pint water
> ice

Mix the fruit juices with water, chill, and serve with generous quantities of ice.

Fruit Cup

Non-alcoholic

> 8 oz diced pineapple (fresh, if possible)
> ½ pint grapefruit juice
> juice of 2 oranges
> juice of 2 lemons
> 2 pints ginger beer
> sugar to taste

Put pineapple cubes in large bowl with a sprinkling of sugar. Pour on the fruit juices, mix well, and add a little more sugar, if desired. Chill this mixture and the bottles of ginger beer separately, add ginger beer just before serving and decorate with fresh mint.

Party Punch

Non-alcoholic.

> (for 50)
> 1 lb sugar
> ½ pint water
> ½ pint freshly made strong tea
> 1 pint fruit syrup
> ½ pint lemon juice
> 1 pint orange juice
> 1 pint pineapple juice
> 6 pints iced water
> ½ bottle maraschino cherries
> 1 large bottle soda water
> mint, orange, lemon and apple garnish

Boil the sugar for 5 minutes in ½ pint of water. Add the tea (strained) fruit syrup and juices. Chill.
Add iced water and soda water, and decorate with mint and slices of fresh orange, lemon and apple.

Epilogue

'My name is Phoebe Hichens and I'm writing a book about winemaking. Can I come and see you?'

I never saw any real reason why the person at the other end of the telephone should respond warmly to this request, but they always did. And when I turned up with my notebook and my questions, even the busy ones – and some, like C. J. Berry, editor of the magazine *Amateur Winemaker* and author of umpteen winemaking classics, were very busy indeed – even they were generous with their time and their knowledge, always managing to tell me the things I needed to know. Indeed Mr Danby, chief chemist at Continental Wine Experts, actually carried out some experiments for me, for which my most grateful thanks. Others gave me golden afternoons, sampling their many splendid wines – I particularly remember those of Arthur and Esmé Wright, and it was no surprise to find their house filled with prizes from winemaking competitions. And Mr and Mrs Arthur Walmsley, recently retired from the Foreign Office, were among the first to show me that good grape wines, such as they had been accustomed to drinking overseas, could be made in England in all of six weeks.

So many people have helped me that it would need another book to write my acknowledgements in full. Winemaking must be one of the most agreeable subjects in the world to research; and apart from new friends, made in the course of so-called business, I have to thank all the old ones who could never come to my home without being presented with yet another experiment, yet another vintage, yet another 'blind' wine-tasting session. When I spoke in Chapter 5 of getting help from your friends, I was thinking very much of my own.

My local wine merchants in Banbury, S. H. Jones, produced the most apt quotation with which to conclude, for Professor Saintsbury was certainly describing all the winemakers and wine drinkers who contributed to this book when he wrote . . .

'. . . that alcoholic liquors have been used by the strongest, wisest, handsomest and in every way best races of man.'

Liquid Capacity

1 gallon = 4·546 litres (or 4546 millilitres)
1 pint = 568 millilitres (ml for short)
½ pint = 284 ml
1 fluid ounce = 28 ml
½ fluid ounce (or 1 tablespoon) = 15 ml (approx.)
¼ fluid ounce (or 1 dessertspoon) = 10 ml (approx.)
⅛ fluid ounce (or 1 teaspoon) = 5 ml (approx.)

Weight

5 lbs = 2·267 kilogrammes
4 lbs = 1·814 kilos
3 lbs = 1·360 kilos
2 lbs = 907 grammes (or gms)
1 lb = 453 gms
½ lb = 226 gms
¼ lb = 113 gms
1 oz = 30 gms (approx.)
½ oz (or 1 tablespoon) = 15 gms (approx.)
¼ oz (or 1 dessertspoon) = 10 gms (approx.)
⅛ oz (or 1 teaspoon) = 5 gms (approx.)

One is almost bound to do a bit of rounding up or rounding down in one's mind simply because this makes the figures so much easier to remember. It's easier, for example, to think of a gallon as 'nearly five litres' or 5 lbs as 'just over 2 kilos' rather than hold the precise figure, 4·546 litres, or 2·267 kilos, in one's head.

So far as winemaking is concerned, this is not likely to cause trouble, for slight inaccuracies in the quantity of water or amount of sugar should not lead to disaster.

Glossary

In this glossary I have not confined myself to the words used in this book. Winemaking has its own jargon and – without getting into the more rarefied vocabulary – the object here is to give you a good working knowledge of the most widely used beer and winemaking terms.

ACETIFICATION A process that turns wine into vinegar. It is caused by bacteria which infects the wine. The process cannot be reversed. (*See* VINEGAR FLY).

AIRLOCK Also called a fermentation trap. This is a device which seals off wine from the outside air, but allows the escape of the carbon dioxide gas generated by fermentation, usually by allowing it to bubble up through water contained in the trap.

AMMONIUM PHOSPHATE A chemical used to stimulate the yeast and usually referred to as yeast nutrient.

ATTENUATION The drop in the level of sugar during fermentation as it is converted to alcohol.

AUTOLYSIS When a yeast cell dies, it releases nitrogen which can be used by other living yeast cells. This process is called autolysis.

BOTTOMS Deposits of yeast and solids formed during fermentation.

BUNG A rubber stopper, in the shape of a cork. A bung with a hole in the middle, into which the airlock fits, is called a pierced bung.

BURTON WATER Very 'hard' (i.e. calcium rich) water such as that found at Burton-on-Trent, which is ideal for brewing pale ales.

CALCIUM SULPHATE ($CaSO_4$) A chemical used to make water 'harder'. It is also called gypsum.

CAMPDEN TABLET A tablet that gives off SULPHUR DIOXIDE and helps to sterilise wine.

CARBON DIOXIDE (CO_2) The gas given off by fermenting wine.

CARBOY A glass container for storing (and making) wine.

CITRIC ACID An important element in achieving a balanced wine. (Too little can result in a very flat taste.) It is found naturally in most fruits, and can also be bought in a prepared form.

DIASTASE An enzyme in barley which converts starch into fermentable sugar.

ETHYL ALCOHOL (C_2H_5OH) The alcohol created by the interaction of yeast and sugar.

FERMENTATION The working together of yeast and sugar to produce alcohol and carbon dioxide.

FERMENTATION LOCK or TRAP *See* AIRLOCK

FILTER A device to trap haze-forming particles in wine. Either paper or pads can be used.

FININGS An ingredient like ISINGLASS or simple egg whites which are added to clear the wine.

FLOGGER A wooden tool for banging in corks.

FORTIFICATION Increasing the strength of wine by the addition of spirits.

FRETTING A 'fretting' wine means a fermenting wine.

FRUCTOSE *See* INVERT SUGAR

GRAVITY, SPECIFIC The density of a liquid, that is, its weight compared to the same volume of pure water. As increasing the sugar content increases the specific gravity the sugar content can be measured by measuring the specific gravity with a HYDROMETER.

GRIST Malting barley after it has been malted and crushed.

GRIT Any grain used in brewing (other than barley).

GYPSUM *See* CALCIUM SULPHATE.

HYDROMETER An instrument for measuring the density (specific gravity) or sugar content of a liquid.

INVERT SUGAR This is sugar that has been split into two component parts – glucose and fructose. Conversion to alcohol only becomes possible when this split has been achieved. Honey and grape sugar are both natural inverts. *See also* INVERTASE.

INVERTASE An enzyme that splits sugar into two component parts, glucose and fructose.

ISINGLASS Originally made from a purified fish gelatine extracted from the swim bladders of sturgeon. *See also* FININGS.

KILN An oven or heated chamber used for drying malt.

KRAUSENING This means adding some vigorously fermenting beer to another which has nearly fermented out.

LEES *See* BOTTOMS.

LONDON WATER Soft water, comparable to water found in the London area, suitable for brown ales and stouts.

MALO-LACTIC FERMENTATION This is a very late fermentation – usually happening after the wine has been bottled, and perhaps as long as a year after it was originally made. In general, it improves the taste of the wine, particularly white wine, as it reduces acidity, and adds freshness and sparkle.

MALT EXTRACT A malt syrup in which the starch has been converted to fermentable sugar.

MASH The mixture of malt and hot water plus any other ingredients which go to make beer.

METABISULPHATE A sterilising chemical that can be used in powder form or in CAMPDEN TABLETS.

MUST The mixture of ingredients (including water) from which a wine is made.

NUTRIENT *See* AMMONIUM PHOSPHATE.

NOGGIN A quarter pint.

OXIDATION Exposure to oxygen. Wine which has been exposed to the air is 'oxidised'.

PECTIN HAZE This is a cloudiness in the wine caused by tiny undissolved particles. It is especially common in wines made from fruits with stones, like peaches or cherries. It can be improved with PECTOZYME.

PECTOZYME A chemical added to the must before fermentation which helps dissolve haze-forming particles.

PECTOLYTIC ENZYME *See* PECTOZYME.

PRESSING Extracting juice from fruit or vegetables.

PRIMING Adding a small quantity of sugar to a bottle of beer, thus causing a slight secondary fermentation which makes the beer tingle and sparkle.

PROOF Proof spirit contains 57·1% alcohol. When a bottle of whisky or gin describes itself as 70° proof, it means it contains 70% proof spirit, which in turn means 40% pure alcohol.

PULP FERMENTATION Fermenting not just with liquid, but with solid particles of fruit or vegetables.

RACKING Siphoning or pouring the wine from one container into another, leaving any deposit or BOTTOMS behind.

ROPINESS Certain bacilli can string together to form 'ropes' in the wine. This may not affect the taste or smell but looks unattractive. It can usually be cured by CAMPDEN TABLETS.

SIPHON A tube for transferring wine from one container to another (RACKING) without tilting and pouring.

STABLE A wine is 'stable' when there is no further danger of fermentation. Stabilising agents are chemicals which prevent further fermentation.

SULPHUR DIOXIDE (SO_2) This is a sterilising agent. It is given off by CAMPDEN TABLETS and METABISULPHATE as they dissolve, killing off bacteria.

SULPHITING You sulphite a wine when you supply it with carbon dioxide – usually in the form of CAMPDEN TABLETS.

STUCK FERMENTATION A fermentation where the yeast has become inactive before it has finished its job.

TANNIN This substance occurs naturally in the skins and stems of fruit, particularly red fruit, and can also be synthesised. It is a vital ingredient in wines like claret, but the immediate taste is harsh. Wines with a high tannin content require a long period of maturing.

VINEGAR FLY This small fly can introduce an infection into wine that will turn it into vinegar. An AIRLOCK is the best defence.

VITICULTURE The cultivation of grape vines.

WORT The combination of ingredients for beer-making before fermentation.

Index

Acidity, 130
Advanced Winemaking, 124–38
Ageing of wines, 129
Airlocks, general information, 29
Alcohol, measurement of, 34 *and see*
    Hydrometer
Ales *see* Beers
Apple Crumble, 168
Apple wine *see* Cider

Bacteria, 40
Barrels *see* Casks
Basic winemaking method, 18
Beaujolais 1, 59
           2, 60
Beef Casserole, 163
Beers: general information, 140–2
    Bitter, Medium, 143
    Bitter, Mild, 146
    Bitter, Strong, 145
    Beer and Brandy Punch, 174
    Brown Ale, 146
    Cock Ale, 148
    Lager, 149
    Stouts, 147
Benedictine, 122
Bishop, The, 173
Black Beauty, 181
Blackcurrant Cooking Wine, 156
Blending: general information, 49–50, 52
    advanced, 86–7
    wine, red, 53
    wine, white, 54
Bottling, 35, 128
Brandy, Poor Man's, 118
    in recipes, 169, 170
    in party drinks,
    peach 119
Brewing, 140
Bungs, 30
Burgundy 1, 61
           2, 62
    in party drinks, 172

Campari 'cheat', 110
Campden tablets, general information, 30
Casks, 125–7
    casks, cleaning, 126
Casserole, Beef, 163
Chablis 1, 77
         2, 78
Champagne 1, 81
              2, 82
    advanced, 136
    cup, 176
Cherry Brandy, 119
Cherry Punch, 174
Chianti 1, 65
          2, 66
Chicken Liver Pâté, 160
Chocolate Cream, 169
Christmas Cordial, 175
Cider, 142, 150
Claret 1, 63
         2, 64
    advanced, 132
Cock Ale, 148
Concentrates, 19–24
Conversion Tables, 184
Cooking wines: introduction, 152–3
    elderberry, 154
    elderflower, 155
    blackcurrant, 156
    orange and rosehip, 157
    rosé, 158
Creme de Menthe, 121
Cups, 175–178, 180, 181

Daily wine 1, 46
            2, 51
            3, 53
Disinfectants, 30, 41
Distilling, 92–4
Dubonnet 'cheat', 110
    in Dubonnet cocktail, 177
    used in blending, 44–5

Elderberry Cooking Wine, 154
Elderflower Cooking Wine, 155
Equipment: advanced, 125
   basic, 27
   stockists, 36

Fermentation: general information, 16, 34
   'stuck', 39
Filters, 31, 97, 129
Finings, 31
Fizziness, adding, 83
Flavourings, 113, 118
Fortified wines: introduction, 96–102
   in party drinks, 172–82
   Madeira, 109
   Port, 108–9
   Port, advanced, 138
   Sherry, 104–7
   Sherry, advanced, 131
   Vermouth, 103
'Freezer method', 93–4, 113–4
Fruit Cup, 181

Gazpacho, 162
Gin, Poor Man's, 115
   in Gin Fizz, 176
Gin Fizz, 176
Ginger Beer, 179
   in Sherry Shiver, 175
Graves 1, 75
   2, 76

Hamburgers, Marinated, 166
Hare, Jugged, 164–5
Heaters, 30
Hock 1, 69
   2, 70
Honey, 45, 58, 100
Hydrometer: general information, 33
   applications in advanced winemaking, 97–100,
   129
Hygiene, 41

Immersion Heaters, 30
Infections, bacterial, 40
Invert sugar, 57, 100–1

Jelly, Wine, 167
Jugged Hare, 164–5

Kedgeree on Wine Rice, 165
Kidneys with Wine Gravy, 166

Lager, 149
Law, the, Home Winemakers and, 92–4
Liebfraumilch 1, 73
   2, 74
   advanced, 134
Liners, 17
Liqueurs: Benedictine, 122
   Cherry Brandy, 119
   Creme de Menthe, 121
   Peach Brandy, 119
   Pineapple Brandy, 120
   Sloe Gin, 121

Madeira, 109
Malts, 140–2
Marinated Hamburgers, 166
Measurements, 184
Metric Tables, 184
Milk Stout, 147
Mistletoe Mull, 172
Moselle 1, 71
   2, 72
Moules Marinières, 161
Mulled Wines, 172, 173, 174

Non-alcoholic drinks, 181–2

Orange and Rosehip Cooking Wine, 157
Orange Sun, 180
Oyster Dip, 162

Party drinks, 172–82
Party Punch, 182
Peach Brandy, 119
Peach, Simple, 167
Pectozyme, 29
Pineapple Brandy, 120
Pink Peach, 180

Port 1, 108
    2, 109
    advanced, 138
    in party drinks, 173
Potato and Salami Soup, 159
Polish Spirit, 111, 113
Proof Spirit, 96

Racking, 127
Records, 35
Red Wines: Claret, 1, 63
              2, 64
    Claret (advanced), 132
    Beaujolais, 59–60
    Burgundy, 61–62
    Chianti, 65–66
    in recipes, 160, 163–166
    in party drinks, 172–80
Regional wines, 56–84
Retsina, 84
Rosé Wines: 1, 67
          2, 68
    cooking rosé, 158
    in recipes, 162, 169
    in party drinks, 172–80
Rosehip and Orange Cooking Wine, 157
Rum, Poor Man's, 118

Sausages au Vin, 163
Sauternes: 1, 79
         2, 80
    in party drinks, 175
Sherry: advanced, 131
    cream, 107
    dry, 104
    medium, 106
    Sherry Ice Cream, 170
    Sherry Shiver, 175
Simple Peach, 167
Siphoning, 28
Sloe Gin, 121
Sodastream, 83
Sparkle, adding, 83
Sparklets, 83
Sparkling wines: champagne, 81, 82, 136
    rosé, 68
    in party drinks, 172–80

Spirits: general information, 92–4, 96, 112–4
    Poor Man's Brandy, 118
    Poor Man's Gin, 115
    Poor Man's Rum, 118
    Poor Man's Whisky, 116
Sterilization, 41, 126
Stouts, 147
Strawberry Cream Shortcake, 169
Strawberry Fare, 177
Strong Bitter, 145
Submersible Heaters, 30
Sugar: feeding method, 97
    sugar, grape, 19
    sugar, invert, 57, 100–1
    syrup, 118
Summer drinks, 175–80
Summer Spice, 178

Tannin, 56, 130
Temperature: general information, 17, 40
    and see Heaters
Tuna Salad, 160

Vermouth: dry, 103
    sweet, 103
Vin Ordinaire *see* Daily Wine
Vinegar Fly, 40

Wheat Wine, 116
Whisky, Poor Man's, 116
White Wines: blending wine, 54
    Chablis, 77, 78
    Graves, 75, 76
    Hock, 69, 70
    Liebfraumilch, 73, 74, 134
    Moselle, 71, 72
    Sauternes, 79, 80
    in recipes, 159–163, 165, 167–168
Wine Cups, 175–178, 180, 181
Wine Jelly, 167
Wines, Mulled, 172, 173, 174, 180
Wine Rice, Kedgeree, 165
Winter drinks, 172–175, 180

Yeasts: general information, 16, 17, 28
    special, 130